Friendly Fetish

A BEGINNER'S GUIDE TO KINK

Emily Dubberley

PIATKUS

PIATKUS

First published in Great Britain in 2009 by Piatkus
Copyright © 2009 by Emily Dubberley

A CIP catalogue record for this book
is available from the British Library

ISBN 978-0-7499-2974-9

Typeset in Adobe Garamond by Phoenix Photosetting, Chatham, Kent
Printed and bound in Great Britain by Clays Ltd, St Ives

Papers used by Piatkus are natural, renewable and recyclable
products sourced from well-managed forests and certified
in accordance with the rules of the Forest Stewardship Council.

Mixed Sources
Product group from well-managed
forests and other controlled sources
www.fsc.org Cert no. SGS-COC-004081
© 1996 Forest Stewardship Council
FSC

Page 44: Quote from *Private Thoughts* by Wendy Maltz and Suzie Boss,
pg. 130, BookSurge 2008, www.BookSurge.com.

Piatkus
An imprint of
Little, Brown Book Group
100 Victoria Embankment
London EC4Y 0DY

An Hachette UK Company
www.hachette.co.uk

www.piatkus.co.uk

To Sam Eddison, for accepting me just the way I am

Contents

Acknowledgements — viii

Introduction — 1

1. Fantasies and Role Play — 11

2. Voyeurism and Exhibitionism — 53

3. Food Play — 91

4. Kinky Props and Fetish Fashion — 123

5. Spanking — 183

6. Bondage — 197

7. Submission, Domination and Beyond — 215

8. Group Sex — 243

Conclusion — 267

Resources — 269

Index — 274

Acknowledgements

Writing about kinky sex is something that some people are judgemental about, so I'm incredibly grateful to my mum for never having an issue with my choice of career and being utterly supportive from day one. Thanks are also due to Sarah Hedley, for devising the 'Emily-at-Large' column that led to some of my wilder experiences, and all of the organisations and individuals that let me enter their world, despite the risk that I might have been one of those bad journalists who's just looking for a salacious story. These include AdultAdventures.co.uk, Mistress Absolute, Pedestal, Splosh Studios, Starkers Naked Disco, Girlskissing.co.uk, Brighton Body Casting, Tawse.com and Nua, to name just a few.

I've also had help from numerous experts and friends, whether in the form of sharing kinky stories, teaching me some of their wilder tricks or simply providing me with cocktails or a hug when I was in need of a break. These include Jenny Ardley, Aimee Davies, Dossie Easton, Mark Farley, Alyson Fixter, Mat Fraser, Emma Gold, Mistress Grace, Lyla Graves, Ashley Hames, Ewan Kirkland, Sarah 'Bird' Lewis, Henry Milliner, Veronica Monet, Nic Ramsay, Annie Sprinkle, Dr Pam Spurr and Wes Stanton.

And of course, thanks have to go to Helen Stanton and Denise Dwyer for helping to make this book a reality – and get people to read it – and my lovely agent Chelsey Fox for all her support and encouragement from my first book to the present day.

Introduction

For many people, the word 'fetish' conjures up images of weedy men in rubber suits, whip-wielding women in thigh-high boots and seedy clubs full of people doing unspeakable things to each other with strangely shaped devices. While there are certainly clubs on the fetish scene that offer that sort of experience, it does fetish – and fetishists – a disservice to assume that it's something that only a few people with niche tastes can enjoy.

Fetish is increasingly entering the mainstream. Hollywood blockbusters such as *Secretary*, *Shortbus* and *The Notorious Betty Page* have explored themes of submission and domination, group sex and foot fetishism. The catwalk is full of bondage and fetish-inspired clothing. Television shows feature almost every kind of kink available, from watersports in *Sex and the City*, to sex with rubber dolls in *Boston Legal* and going to wild orgies in *Nip/Tuck*. But if a 'normal' couple likes the idea of experimenting with fetish, the whole scene can feel intimidating. Gimp masks, fearsome Dominatrixes and unpleasant-looking metal instruments can all make a beginner think it's far too scary and opt to skip the sexual exploration thing altogether.

Some fetishists can be disparaging about 'vanillas' (people who don't indulge in kinky sex of any kind, instead preferring their sex without any 'flavouring'), making it hard for people to explore their desires in a non-threatening way. And then there's the issue of society deeming anyone who is overtly sexual as a 'pervert', which can, again, make it hard to summon up the confidence to explore your darker desires. Even knowing which books, magazines or websites to choose should you want to learn more is a minefield, most of the material out there being firmly targeted at the fetish devotee rather than people with a casual interest in enhancing their sex life.

As a full-time sex writer, I'm lucky enough to have spent a fair chunk of the last seven years involved in the fetish arena, without actually being a permanent participant in it. In addition to reading hundreds of books about every aspect of sexual exploration, I've immersed myself in numerous different 'scenes' (fetishistic experiences) as part of my job. I've given advice to women at orgies who didn't set ground rules with their partner beforehand and, as a result, felt heartbroken as they watched their man getting it on with another woman. I've had a positive naturist experience at a naked disco, in which everyone was wonderfully respectful (even if there were 400 men there and only three women), and a tear-inducing naturist experience at a resort in which the men were obese, twice my age and lecherous, and the tour rep wore an 'FBI: Female Body Inspector' T-shirt. I've had my genitals cast in plaster of Paris, externally, internally and while having sex with my partner; attended spanking, dirty talk and tantric masterclasses; and tested over 500 sex toys of numerous types.

One of my favourite experiences was an evening at a female domination club, in which men acquiesced to my every whim whether it was peeling me a grape, getting me a drink or lying down to be trampled while I wore my highest heels (OK, I admit – I was asked to trample the slave, rather than deciding it was something that I particularly wanted to do; but it was certainly a liberating experience). And I've often been to Europe's biggest sex party, Night of the Senses (which raises money for Outsiders, a charity that helps disabled people find partners, and just goes to prove that there's more than one side to fetish events). There, I described the outrageous sexual scenes before me to a blind guy, while eyeing up a hot bloke with thalidomide, and witnessing people having public sex, playing in the dungeon and generally letting their kinky selves roam free.

In short, I've experienced almost every aspect of fetish, thanks to the (largely) lovely people who've been kind enough to let me inside their world. And OK, along the way I've picked up a few kinky tricks that have certainly enhanced my sex life, without plunging me into a hedonistic world of debauchery (other than on particularly good nights, of course). I don't see fetish as an integral part of my life, but it's certainly something I'm glad I've explored because it's allowed me to pick and choose the parts that have been fun or educational and use them to benefit my sex life.

Having amassed a huge amount of information about the fetish world, and seen that world being misrepresented again and again as threatening, morally dubious or just plain weird, it made sense to me to set the record straight. And because I've tried so many things, I can pass on that knowledge in such a way that you can try any level of fetish safely, without actually having to experience everything that I have unless you really want to.

Friendly Fetish aims to bust the myths that people are purely 'vanilla' or 'kinky', and that exploring your fetishes makes you a pervert. From introducing fantasies to dabbling with food play, exploring submission and domination to tying your lover up with aplomb, it tells you everything in simple terms, so that you know what's what and can decide whether you'd like to give it a go. Each kink is illustrated with case studies, true stories from some of my wilder adventures and tips from some of my kinkier friends, providing a comprehensive guide to what to expect without having to don a single piece of rubber (unless you want to).

Whether you're curious about nibbling food off your lover's nether regions, fancy being tied up and teased for hours on end or could think of nothing hotter than seeing your partner in a saucy outfit, *Friendly Fetish* offers a no-holds-barred insight into the fetish world, and will help you see that there's nothing to be scared of: it's all good, dirty fun.

So What is Fetish?

Technically speaking, a fetish is 'any object or non-genital part of the body that causes a habitual erotic response or fixation'. Sexy, eh? Basically, what this means is that someone can only get aroused if a particular item is involved in their sex play, for example a pair of high-heeled shoes, a rubber catsuit or a bunch of balloons (yes, seriously). This is where the idea of fetishists being dodgy perverts who require a host of props before they can even think about getting off comes from. While that's obviously a load of nonsense, a pure fetishist won't find sexual satisfaction merely from the touch of a lover, which means that they may miss out on a lot of fun.

However, nowadays the words fetish and kink tend to be used interchangeably to refer to any sex act that is outside the norm (although given the number of people who practise some form of kinky sex, it's hard to say exactly what 'normal' is any more). For the purposes of this book, the words fetish and kink are both used to describe the host of sexual delights that are available when you open your mind and are prepared to entertain new ideas, rather than the definition given above. It may not be strictly accurate, but it covers a multitude more sins (and pleasures) than the technical description allows.

Is Fetish Normal?

It may come as a surprise, but if you bumped into most fetishists outside a fetish club, you'd be hard pushed to label them as such. Although some people wear their fetishes on their sleeve by incorporating collars or piercings, branding or rubber-wear into their everyday look, the vast majority of people keep their kinks to themselves, only letting that side of themselves show when with a partner or other fetishists. As such, your postman (or partner) is as likely to be a fetishist as the punk you see on public transport who you think looks a bit intimidating.

According to research from Queendom.com, 24 per cent of people find the idea of watching someone else have sex with their partner arousing, 40 per cent have tried BDSM (bondage and discipline, dominance and submission, and sadism and masochism), 50 per cent would like to try group sex and 92 per cent use fantasy when they masturbate (and these are just a few of the kinks that are out there).

By the time you factor in dressing up in rubber, PVC or role-play outfits, foot fetishism, finding women in stockings sexy, gender play, using sex toys, having sex in front of other people, spanking and messing around with food, almost everyone has a kink of some kind. And while men are statistically more likely to have, say, a foot fetish or rely on some 'non-sexual' stimuli such as thigh-high boots, all you need to do is look at the number of women who coo over Manolos or get frisky when they share their fantasies with a lover to see that fetish is by no means gender-specific.

As such, that means that you're probably more 'normal' if you spend your weekends trussed up while your partner spanks you than if you never experiment with anything beyond missionary-style sex. That doesn't mean that fetish has to be a part of your sex life in order for you to have a good time between the sheets. However, it's nothing to be ashamed of and can certainly add colour to your sex life.

The Pros and Cons of Kink

As with anything, there are pros and cons to getting kinky. Some kinks have no risks at all other than the chance that you may end up giggling with your partner, which is no bad thing. Others, at the wilder end of the spectrum, have specific guidelines that need to be followed for your safety. All of these will be outlined as we go along, but don't forget to take into account your own comfort levels every step of the way. There's no point engaging in any sexual act just for the sake of it, or because you feel you 'should' in order to be sexually adventurous. Just as we all like different things to eat and drink, we all like different sexual acts and experiences, so tailor everything to your own level and pace: *your* sex life is *your* decision.

Similarly, if your partner dislikes the idea of doing something that you are keen on, don't pressure them. Sex is about two people (or more) not just one, so there's no point engaging in any act unless everyone concerned is comfortable with the idea. Hell, if your partner's open to the concept, you can always just talk dirty about what you want instead.

On the plus side, experimenting with different fetishes can help to prevent you from falling into a relationship rut by keeping your sex life fresh. The more you explore your sexuality, the more likely you are to find something that gives you the ultimate thrill. And in some cases, fetish can even help you to find a mojo you thought was long since gone.

How to Use This Book

While the different types of fetish covered in individual chapters do have specific rules, by far the most important set of rules to establish is your own. Before you read on, have a think about anything that you would or wouldn't be prepared to try. Look through the Contents list at the beginning of the book if you're not sure where to start, but don't limit yourself purely to the chapter titles. Think about whether you feel comfortable with the idea of taunting a partner or being taunted; of giving or receiving pain; of piercings and tattoos; or even the concept of sharing your darkest thoughts with a partner. There's no right or wrong: there's simply your own way, so be certain you know what that is before you start to play.

This book aims to be accessible to everyone, and if you've bought it purely to figure out how to share your fantasies with your partner and with no intention of getting into submission, domination or spanking, that's all well and good. Conversely, if you're already pretty kink-conversant and want to push your limits further there should also be information here that will help you safely on your way. Don't cast your rules in stone – there's always room for change – but *do* work out where your current comfort levels are before you start exploring your sexuality with your partner. You can always amend your list of rules if you change your mind at a later date.

Friendly Fetish is designed to be used however you see fit. It starts with kinks that some people may perceive to be at the lighter end of the spectrum and builds up to some of the more extreme fetishes. If you're a beginner, it's probably advisable to start at the beginning and only continue through the book as and when you feel ready: unless of course, you discover that you're a natural kinkster, and want to explore every joy that the fetish world has to offer as soon as you possibly can.

Alternatively, you can pick and choose those chapters and topics that most appeal to you: it takes different strokes for different folks (some like hard strokes, while others would flinch at even the mildest dusting with a horsetail whip), so don't assume that you'll enjoy every sex act in this book: there are certainly some things I've tried that I've filed strictly under 'experience' and wouldn't want to do again – and I was getting paid for it!

Personal rules aside, as an overall guideline when experimenting with any kind of kink, all acts should be 'safe, sane and consensual'. This means learning about any physical and emotional risks entailed in the games you choose to play, having a 'safe word' for any kind of power play (of which more later) and only playing with people who are equally willing to experiment. And note that 'consensual' refers to informed consent, so you shouldn't use drink or drugs to lower someone's defences or try to manipulate a partner into doing something that you know, deep down, they don't want to do.

Only enter into fetish if it's something that you're sure you want to do and your partner is equally curious. While the hints and tips in this book will prove invaluable on your journey, entering into kinky sex is entirely at your own risk because only you know your personal limits.

Some fetishes do carry physical and emotional risks, though again, these can easily be avoided by following safety guidelines. Also, becoming too dependent on fetish can mean it gets in the way of intimacy, with props and equipment becoming more important than bonding with your partner (which is, after all, what having sex in a relationship is all about).

If anything distressing does crop up (no pun intended) as a result of fetish play unearthing bits of your psyche you'd forgotten all about, there is a host of counsellors out there who can help you work through your issues. And it can be a valuable self-development tool even if things don't go exactly the way you'd imagined they might.

But when all is said and done, kinky sex isn't really all that different from 'vanilla' sex. It's simply a new way to bond with your partner, have orgasms and explore your sexuality.

And whether you've kept your darkest fantasies to yourself or are already beginning to explore your kinkier side, *Friendly Fetish* will guide you through the wonderfully decadent world that is kink.

So, what are you waiting for? Prepare to have your mind opened and to experience your wildest dreams coming true.

CHAPTER ONE

Fantasies and Role Play

If you're new to kinky sex, it makes sense to begin by getting in touch with your fantasies. After all, it's only by knowing what turns you on that you can take things to the next level and start experimenting. Some people have complex, highly evolved fantasies, while others may think about nothing more than the way their lover looks wearing a particular outfit. Neither is 'right' or 'wrong'. It's simply down to what turns you on.

Some of the most common fantasies for men and women alike include:

- submission (being the passive partner in sex)

- domination (telling your partner what to do)

- exhibitionism (showing off your body to other people)

- voyeurism (observing other people in a state of undress or while having sex)

- seducing a stranger

- group sex

- playing a particular character during sex (such as the naughty nurse or high-class gigolo).

Some people have a host of different fantasies covering a multitude of sins (or rather pleasures), while others tend to have just the one fantasy or variations on the same theme. There's no need to feel nervous about exploring your fantasies. As well as being fun it can also be a valuable seduction tool – telling your lover that you've spent the day indulging in self-pleasure while thinking about them is bound to be an ego boost, after all. So just tap into your erotic imagination and let it flow.

What Are Fantasy and Role Play?

Fantasy and role play are often lumped into the same category as they both involve using your imagination to enhance your sex life. However, while the former relies on thoughts alone, the latter can involve outfits, props, different locations and even scripts if you take it to its fullest level.

Pretty much everyone has some form of sexual fantasy, even if they don't admit it. According to psychologists Bruce Ellis and Donald Symons, men are more than twice as likely as women to report having sexual fantasies at least once a day and fantasise about a greater number of different partners. They are also much more likely than women to report having had sexual fantasies about more than a thousand different people in the course of their lives. However, that doesn't mean that sexual fantasy is exclusively the preserve of men. Nancy Friday's book *My Secret Garden* (1973) showed the immense breadth of women's sexual fantasies, ranging from traditional romantic daydreams to graphic fantasies involving a cast of thousands, with the pet dog thrown in for good measure.

While some people want certain fantasies to come true, it's by no means the case that every fantasy is something that you would necessarily want to be a reality. That's one of the joys of sexual fantasy: you can imagine and get off on sordid acts that you'd never really want to experience in real life, and make sure that everything goes exactly the way that you want it to.

TRUE CONFESSIONS
I LET MY MIND WANDER

It's safe to say that my fantasy life is pretty varied. One night, I'll imagine walking into a room in which everyone finds me compellingly attractive and all are fighting over who will be first to have me, making increasingly erotic promises; another night, I'll be tied down by a masked intruder and made to do everything that he asks of me. Sometimes, I imagine that I'm the star attraction at a slave auction, and at other times, I'll fantasise about being a beautiful princess who's being prepared for a handsome sheikh by a roomful of handmaidens. In reality, I'm very happy with the gentle, loving sex that I have with my husband and would never want to cheat on him, but I figure that what goes on in my mind is my business and if I want to let it wander, then so be it. I know that he has fantasies too – I've found some of the magazines that he reads and doesn't think I know about – but that's entirely up to him.

Lydia, 35, pharmacist

Why have fantasies?

Fantasies are a fantastic way to explore different sides of your sexual persona. In the same way that you wear different 'masks' with different people, being the child, colleague or friend depending on who you are talking to, fantasy allows you to explore the libertarian, the submissive, the exhibitionist and numerous other aspects of your sexual make-up. That's not to say that everyone's sexual persona incorporates all of these, but chances are that if you examine your fantasies, you'll realise how multi-faceted you are.

By indulging in fantasy play you can delve into different personas, some of whom may enjoy different sexual experiences from the 'normal' you: for example, a woman who tends to only like sex in the missionary position may prefer hard and fast doggy-style sex if she assumes a submissive role. A man who loves quickie-style instant gratification may revel in being tied up and teased for hours if he's playing a 'captured spy'. The mind is a powerful thing and can have a surprisingly significant impact on your sex life. And if you share your many sexual personas with your partner, you're far less likely to fall into a rut because one night you'll be a shy and retiring librarian who has to be coaxed out of her shell, and the next you'll be the whip-cracking Dominatrix who's demanding at least an hour of cunnilingus before releasing her 'slave'.

Your fantasies will also open up new physical experiences, as there's a specific type of orgasm that can be experienced with no physical contact, using nothing more than the power of your mind. Called the 'psycholagnic orgasm', it's achieved by focusing on erotic thoughts rather than physical sensations. Although it's more common in women than in men, it's certainly true that both genders can become aroused by words and thoughts alone: why else would phone sex lines be so popular?

Achieving a psycholagnic orgasm

If you like the idea of a psycholagnic orgasm, start off by relaxing. Orgasm is always much easier when you're not stressed, so allowing yourself time to chill out after a hard day will increase your chances of reaching climax. Take a long bath with aromatherapy oils and candles, play some music that helps you kick back, massage your partner and get them to do the same to you, all the while flirting with each other, and you'll soon find yourself getting into the mood. Once you're feeling calmly content, introduce some sexy talk into the equation (*see* 'Ultimate talking-dirty tips', p. 20). Agree with your partner that, for the first hour at least, you won't touch each other's genitals or nipples. You can hold each other, kiss each other and massage each other in a non-sexual way as you talk, but it's the words that are the arousal tool here, rather than any physical contact. Indeed, the less physical contact you allow each other, the more you are likely to crave it, particularly when things start hotting up.

Aim for an equal balance of talk between you, rather than one of you giving a monologue about your sexual fantasies; that way, you'll connect with each other a lot more. However, if you can, feed into each other's fantasies. If you learn that your partner loves the idea of being dominated, for example, throw some of that into the equation; if stockings are a turn-on, mention that you're going to be wearing them later; and if certain sex acts always get your lover hot, make sure that you include those in the erotic story you're developing together.

There's no guarantee that sharing fantasies will result in a psycholagnic orgasm, but by entering into your fantasies you can help yourself evolve sexually, have foreplay in public by whispering kinky suggestions into each other's ears and intensify your orgasms. Given all those benefits, it only makes sense to give it a go. All you have to fear is your own inhibitions.

Facing your fears

Despite sexual fantasy having been in the public domain for over thirty years, some people still feel uncomfortable about admitting that they have them. Indeed, according to the website Queendom.com, only 53 per cent of women and 62 per cent of men claim to have no shame about their sexual fantasies at all. Luckily, only 3 per cent of women and 2 per cent of men are ashamed of most of their fantasies but that still leaves well over a third of us feeling uncomfortable about some aspects of our fantasy life. This is a negative and pointless perspective. Fantasy and reality are two entirely different things, and there's no reason to feel guilty about doling out evil punishments to a 'slave' in your head (indeed, there's no reason to feel guilty about living out such experiences in real life, as long as the slave consents).

If you feel uncomfortable about some of your fantasies, try to work out why. Is it because you're naturally meek but assume a dominant persona when it comes to your sexual fantasies, and that makes you feel uncomfortable? Did your parents tell you that sex is bad and wrong? Or is your partner so used to you fitting into one particular sexual mould that you are worried they'll think badly of you if you confess to having different desires?

Whatever the reason, it's worthwhile dealing with it (through counselling if need be) so that you can accept your sexuality in all its forms. You don't have to share all of your fantasies with your partner; accepting them is purely about your own happiness and sense of self-worth. However, sharing some of your fantasies with a partner can be a wonderful way to increase the intimacy between you and to learn more about what makes your partner tick.

Introducing Fantasies into Your Relationship

If you've never shared fantasies with your partner before, it can be a bit intimidating at first. Many men and women are too scared to raise their fantasies with their partner, particularly when at the more explicit end of the spectrum. You might worry that your partner is going to judge you negatively, laugh at you or think that you're a pervert. You might be concerned that your partner won't understand where you're coming from if their fantasies are different from yours. Or you could fear that your partner will ask you what inspired a particular fantasy and feel that you have to confess to watching pornography, calling a telephone sex line or, worse, remembering conversations or experiences that you had with an ex.

While all of these things are possibilities, if you're in a loving relationship, with the trust, affection and respect that this entails, sharing your fantasies with a partner will help to build intimacy and, as such, is well worth doing.

There are various ways to approach sharing your fantasies, and, as with everything, the best way to avoid negative consequences is by taking things slowly. If you talk freely and openly about sex with your partner on a regular basis, you could just drop it into conversation. This can either be outside the bedroom, so that you can discuss things in a 'hands off' way, or during sexy talk as a form of foreplay. Either option is valid, but if you go for the latter, *see* 'Ultimate talking-dirty tips', p. 20.

If you find the idea of simply blurting out your innermost desires too intimidating, try taking a softer approach by buying an erotic book that covers a range of fantasies (*see*

Resources, p. 269) and taking it in turns to read to each other. After each fantasy, you can discuss whether or not you find the story arousing. The advantage of using this method is that it creates distance between you and the fantasy, also giving you a chance to gauge your partner's response as you go along, so that you can edit your fantasies as necessary without them ever knowing what you've done. While honesty is important in relationships, you don't have to share every single thought that you have.

Another approach that creates a little distance but also calls for more trust is to write your partner an erotic story detailing your fantasies. You don't need to be a literary genius to do this: just write the way that you speak and your natural 'voice' will come through (spell checkers in Word or similar programmes are a good way to ensure that your story isn't ruined by typos). If you do opt for this method, make sure that you go for the mildest version of your fantasy: if you like the idea of stripping in front of a baying crowd, tone it down into stripping solely for your partner; and if you get aroused at the idea of being tied up and 'punished', start with a mild spanking rather than going straight in with nipple clamps and a cat-o'-nine-tails. This way, you can judge your partner's response to the core idea and assess whether they're likely to be intimidated or turned off if you reach further into the darker echelons of your mind.

Whichever method you choose, it's best if you try to encourage an exchange of fantasies rather than simply telling your partner your own. This has two advantages: firstly, that your partner will be as scared of being judged as you are and, as such, is more likely to go gently when responding to your confession; and secondly, you get to learn about your partner's fantasy life as well as sharing your own, which can only serve to benefit your relationship.

TRUE CONFESSIONS

SHARING FANTASIES GOT US OUT OF A RUT

When I met Karl, we fell in love almost at first sight and had moved in together within three months. At first our sex life was great but as time went on, it decreased. He seemed to lose interest and I found myself retreating more and more into my fantasies when I was on my own and when I was having sex with him. One night, I got a bit tipsy and decided to tell him what I fantasise about. To my surprise, he kept urging me to tell him more and more about it, and even started throwing in a few suggestions of his own, saying things like, 'Does one of the women who's watching come over and sit on your face?' and, 'Is there someone there who's filming what you're doing?' All his suggestions made me hotter than I'd been in months and we ended up having passionate sex.

We talked about it the next day and Karl confessed that he'd thought our sex life was getting a bit predictable and he'd begun to see it as a chore, but that the previous night had felt like the early days again. We decided to go shopping together for some naughty books and read the stories together when we got home. We both found lots of new ideas to turn us on and started incorporating some of them into our sex life – like tying each other up and him spanking me.

It made our sex life so much better. If I feel horny and he's not in the mood, all I have to do now is mention one of our fantasies and he's ready for me. We don't fantasise all the time, and I find it easier to just focus on him when we have sex now because I know that we'll probably share our fantasies the next time we have sex, so I can just enjoy being in the moment when we don't. I wish I'd had the confidence to share my fantasies with him years ago, but at the same time, it's nice that we found a way to bring the honeymoon period of our relationship back again.

Emma, 26, marketing manager

Ultimate talking-dirty tips

Although some people find the phrase 'talking dirty' offensive because it suggests that sex is something sordid and taboo, others find that this is part of the appeal. But whether you call it 'talking dirty', 'sexy talk' or even 'whispering sweet nothings', there are certain tips and tricks that will help you to deliver the ultimate verbal seduction:

- **Talk softly.** Shouting at someone is unlikely to get them aroused. By keeping the volume down, you're making your partner lean closer, focus more on what you're saying and, as a result, they're drawn deeper into your words. It also has the added advantage of lowering your tone of voice (try it if you don't believe me – it's an old radio trick), and a deeper voice gives all of your words a more sensual feel. People tend to find deeper voices more soothing to listen to, and getting your partner into a state of relaxation while you're talking smut will only serve to enhance the experience for both of you.

- **Slow your voice down.** It's rare that you'll hear a woman on a phone sex line talking nineteen to the dozen and that's not just because people pay by the minute. A slow voice is easier to follow and your partner will cling on to your every word, anticipating the next erotic phrase that you're going to utter.

- **Throw in the occasional pause.** This is a good trick, particularly mid-sentence. For example, saying, 'I want to slowly kiss my way down your body, lingering when I get to your inner thighs,' will give your partner a thrill; but if you say, 'I want to slowly kiss my way down your body, lingering when I get to your . . . inner thighs,' chances are their imagination will have raced ahead and they'll already be envisaging you lingering over all manner of different body parts.

- **Don't think too exotic.** You don't have to come up with a host of exotic scenarios when you're talking dirty with your partner. Start with something simple, like telling them what you'd like to do to every inch of their body. Wait until both of you feel comfortable about communicating your sexual desires in this way before you up the gear by introducing new characters, props or scenarios.

- **Talk things through first.** It's worth chatting to each other before you leap into talking dirty to establish whether there are any words that you find a particular turn-on (or -off). When you're immersed in sharing smut, it can be all too easy to kill the mood by using a word that your partner finds ugly, offensive or both. While some women love words and phrases like 'slut', 'whore' or 'bad girl', others will become instantly turned off and feel degraded (and not in a hot and kinky way). Similarly, while some men love the idea of having a 'huge throbbing love machine', others will collapse in laughter at the mere thought. So, work out your lexicon of lust before you move into the mechanics and you're sure to find that words can work wonders for you both.

EMILY'S EXPERIENCES: I LEARNED HOW TO HAVE PHONE SEX FROM THE PROFESSIONALS

When I went on Babestation, I have to confess to being intimidated. Babestation is one of many live phone-in sex lines, with a couple of major differences. Firstly, it's televised, so you can't just sit there in your pyjamas randomly talking filth, safe in the knowledge that you can pretend to be a busty blonde babe, thigh-booted Dominatrix or innocent student, depending on what the caller wants. As such, I'd endured two hours of having my hair teased into porn-star fullness, my breasts boosted with chicken fillets and a push-up bra and my face caked in make-up, until I bore a vague (very vague) resemblance to the twenty-something glamour models around me. Secondly, other people can listen in on the calls (for a premium, of course) so the words I used had to work on multiple men (and the occasional woman) as well as the caller who was paying to speak to me.

Although I write erotica for a living, and have had a fair few salacious conversations with partners, both over the phone and in person, there's a big difference between that and having sexy conversations with strangers who are listening in with their cocks in their hands.

Having been fully briefed on the complex guidelines that rule phone sex lines (no mention of underage activity, religion, animals or any form of illegal sex, which made me feel a lot more comfortable even though it ruled out naughty nuns and saucy schoolgirls) I took to the phone. Oddly, I was more nervous about making sure I wiggled and giggled in the right way, not being overly used to being in front of TV cameras, than I was about talking filth to strangers. Until the phone rang for the first time.

I can't remember his name, but I do recall leading him into a sapphic (lesbian) story, feeling pretty safe that it would get him off as it's such a common male fantasy. My gut instinct proved right. As I related the (entirely fictitious) tale about how 'helpful' one of my fellow Babestation babes had been, massaging body lotion into every inch of my body then helping me slip into skimpy underwear and straightening my stockings (another 'tick' on the male fantasy board), I could hear him panting.

I kept my voice slow and low, making him wait for every breathy word, but was still shocked when, after hearing me say that the Babestation babe had given my pert arse a spank like the cheeky minx she was, he grunted and audibly came. It was loud enough that the other 'babes' in the studio could hear it, and they all bounced up and down on the beds cheering, 'Emily got her first orgasm.' (The studio wasn't miked up so the only words the callers could hear were those spoken down the phone.) That gave me the confidence to continue. In fact, I was a bit disappointed at how easy it had been, as I'd been getting into the story myself, and for the rest of my session, I gave sixteen men orgasms directly and had about the same number again listening in at all times – apparently enough to get me hired. But I declined. While it had been fun, as a full-time job it just wasn't for me.

When not to share your fantasies

While sharing fantasies is generally a good thing, there are certain thoughts that it's best to keep to yourself, not out of dishonesty but because even the most broad-minded partner is likely to feel hurt if you confess.

Generally speaking, it's best to avoid anything that's too 'close to home'. For example, many people fantasise about having sex with their best friend or, worse (from a fantasy-sharing rather than judgemental point of view), their partner's best friend. This is entirely understandable, given that our best friends are generally the people who know us best (second only to our partners, perhaps), and we tend to be friends with people who are similar to ourselves. However, it's likely to introduce jealousy into the relationship if you let slip about your feelings.

These fantasies don't just apply to friends of the opposite sex either: fantasising about a same-sex best friend is relatively common in both men and women. And while men are more likely to be understanding about a woman having same-sex fantasies, it's still rife with risk as the woman may well feel uncomfortable if her partner suggests that she makes her sapphic dream come true, with him watching, of course . . .

Similarly, if you, like many men and women, fantasise about your best friend's partner at least occasionally, that is something best to keep to yourself, particularly if you tend to go out in a group with said best friend and partner. After all, there's nothing to stop your partner from sharing your secret if they've had one drink too many, and that will only lead to trouble. Fantasies about a partner's family member or boss are also best kept within your own imagination. And as to fantasies about an ex-partner, don't even *think* of going there! Most people tend to be at least slightly insecure about the lovers who've 'been there first', not to mention worrying that their partner still has a crush on their old flame(s). This counts doubly if you're still in contact with them. Making a partner feel that they can't compete with one (or all) of your exes is immature and will (rightly) upset them. It may sound obvious but you'd be surprised how many people have made the mistake of telling all in the misguided belief that honesty and full disclosure are the same thing.

Then there's the timing of fantasies. While it's acceptable to fantasise about whatever you want, whenever you want, it's best not to admit to your partner if you're one of the 9 per cent of women or 10 per cent of men who fantasise about another person while having sex with a partner. Even the most sexually confident person may feel their performance is being criticised if their partner is unable to get off without thinking about someone else. It's also human nature to start to compare yourself with the other person and find yourself lacking, should you find out your partner's mind is elsewhere during sex. While sharing fantasies can be a great way to increase the bond between you, admitting that you think about other people when you're being intimate with your partner is liable to have the opposite effect. Although Queendom.com found that 32 per cent of men and 34 per cent of women say that they have no objection to their partner fantasising about someone else during sex, it's only with the proviso that the partner keeps their thoughts to themselves. Given that only 12 per cent of men never substitute or switch partners during the course of a single sexual fantasy, total honesty here is definitely not the way forward.

As a general rule, use your common sense. If the thing that you're confessing to is something you wouldn't want to hear from your partner, it's probably best to keep your lips zipped. Like it or not, most people tend to have at least some jealousy in them, and there's no point in fuelling this by sharing thoughtless fantasies. Keep them to yourself and if your partner asks why you're particularly aroused, smile beguilingly and simply say, 'I've been thinking about you all day, darling.'

TRUE CONFESSIONS

HIS FANTASY SCARED ME

When I was seventeen, I went out with a guy who was quite religious. He didn't believe in sex before marriage, but was happy to fool around. I encouraged him to share his fantasies with me as he'd had quite an uptight upbringing and seemed to believe that sex was bad. This was something I really didn't agree with, and I thought that through talking about sex 'normally' he'd get over some of his issues. I was happy to respect his boundaries, but didn't want him to go around with a negative attitude towards sex as it's something that's important to me.

One day, after work, he was smiling broadly, and I asked him what had put him in such a good mood. He said that his boss had been a real cow all day and had made him really angry, so he'd gone into the toilets and masturbated about doing all kinds of horrible things to her. I found it really woman-hating and told him so, which led to us having a huge row and breaking up.

In hindsight, I'm glad that we did, as I think his upbringing had given him really flawed views about sex. Don't get me wrong: I don't think there's anything wrong with having kinky fantasies, but the idea of masturbating out of anger and directing that towards a woman really scared me.

Ella, 25, computer games designer

Fantasy and Role Play Games

Once you've opened the Pandora's box of fantasy, and hopefully discovered the joy and hope inside it, rather than all the nasties, there are numerous ways that you can use it to enhance your sex life. Phone sex, cybersex, writing each other erotic stories, entering virtual worlds, role playing and even actually enacting fantasies can all be wonderfully liberating if done in the right way. As with anything sexual, just make sure that you talk ideas through with your partner before plunging in: a little talk can stop a lot of complication and upset. But with any luck, entering into your mutual fantasy worlds will only enhance your relationship.

Phone sex

Phones can be used for fantasy sex in a number of ways: through text messages, voice calls or exchanging saucy photographs; you can even attach some phones to mobile-powered discreet vibrators that are set off when the phone rings, and as technology develops, who knows what other options it will bring.

Text-message flirtation is one of the easiest ways to make foreplay last all day without even laying a finger on each other. Start by sending your lover a saucy fantasy-based text message after they've left for work. Make sure that you finish with an open-ended question, so that you're inviting a response explicitly (and indeed, inviting an explicit response). For example, you might write something like, 'When you get home tonight, I'll be wearing stockings, suspenders and a short frilly French maid's outfit. What do you want to do to me . . . ?' With any luck, your partner will respond in kind.

Continue this back-and-forth flirtation until lunchtime, sending as many messages as you both have time for, then take advantage of your lunch break to up the gear with some phone sex.

Find somewhere that you won't be disturbed, then continue the fantasy verbally, having first checked that it's convenient for your partner. Even if they can't respond in kind, it can still be hot thinking about your partner gradually getting more and more aroused at your words, while trying to make their end of the phone call sound 'innocent'.

After lunch, send another saucy message, again leaving it open-ended and continue until it's time to go home. Then run a bath, get dressed up as per your text messages and wait for your lover to arrive. You can be certain that they won't be working late after a day that spicy.

You can also use phone sex as a way to maintain intimacy when you're apart. If you have a long-distance relationship or are going to be spending a significant amount of time away from each other, it's worth investing in a Skype phone so that you can make free phone calls over the Internet. Nothing ruins a hot phone sex session more than the thought of getting a huge bill at the end of the month (well, except for your flatmate, mum or kids walking in when you're midway through describing exactly what you'd like to do with your lover and a jug of warm chocolate sauce).

Don't forget that your phone probably has a camera function too. As such, if you really want to heat things up, you can always nip into the loos at work and send ever-more graphic photographs of yourself as the day progresses, finishing with one in which you are lying in the bath – covered with bubbles, of course – prior to slipping into your erotic outfit. Phone sex is about the tease, after all . . .

TRUE CONFESSIONS
HANGING ON THE TELEPHONE

I've been with my husband Adrian since I was sixteen. Although our sex life was nothing to complain about, we always did the same thing and it wasn't as exciting as it used to be. I thought this was normal because we'd been together for a long time. I also found it hard to tell him what I wanted in bed because, and this may sound weird, I'd known him too long. When he was told that he had to work in an office at the other end of the country for a month, I was actually a bit relieved at the idea of having the flat to myself.

We agreed that we'd talk every day so that the time would pass more quickly. Even though our sex life was hardly sparkling, we really love each other and I didn't like the idea of spending so much time without any contact. For the first few days, our conversations were pretty mundane, but when it rolled around to Sunday morning – our usual time for nookie – he was more romantic than usual, telling me that he really missed me. I joked that he was just missing his morning action and he admitted that he was.

I felt a bit of a tingle at the thought of him sitting there wishing he was with me, thinking about our usual Sunday-morning activities. I didn't feel the usual pressure to go through the motions and told him that I wished he was with me too, and that I'd really like to have him in my mouth. That's something which is strictly for special occasions and I could hear the husk in his voice as he said, 'Really?' I told him that I really missed him and let my intonation suggest the rest. He asked if I was touching myself and I felt another tingle, so replied, 'I am now.' I could hear him groan again and asked if he was doing the same. When he said that he was, I felt really sexy and powerful. I asked him to describe what he was doing, and he did, interspersing his descriptions with asking what I was doing and what I'd like him to do to me. I was more honest than I've ever been before. The distance made it easy to be myself.

From that day onwards, we spoke to each other for hours every night and as soon as he got home, we made love – in the front room rather than the bedroom. Now I sometimes ask him to call me when he's on his way home from work so that we can talk sexily together. I still don't think I could do it face to face – it'd be too embarrassing if he could see me – but phone sex has improved our sex life so much, it's like we're a whole new couple.

Susie, 26, telemarketer

Cybersex

A natural extension or alternative to phone sex, cybersex entails signing up for any of the numerous free messaging services and talking smut to each other over the Internet. This is most definitely best avoided when you're at work, no matter how tempting it may seem if your working day is so dull that solitaire is the only other option to keep your brain engaged. However, if you and your partner are away from each other because you have a long-distance relationship, work from home or work long hours and get home when it's too late to go on a date together, it's a good way to keep your sex life on the boil without any physical contact.

Cybersex allows you to get carried away into your fantasies as you can pretend to be whoever or whatever you want to be. You can even set up different names to sign in with so that your partner knows what kind of fantasy game you want to play. For example, one night you might be ArmyBoy and another night you might choose to be HarshMaster.

Cybersex can also involve webcams, so that you can get dressed up and show your partner that what you are saying is, indeed, truthful. However, from a security point of view it makes sense to keep your head and any other identifiable features (such as distinctive tattoos) out of shot. You don't want someone hacking into your account and broadcasting images of you playing the perfect wanton wench over the Internet. And you can always give your partner the full picture when you next meet up . . .

TRUE CONFESSIONS
HE MADE ME CLICK MY MOUSE

I've been single for two years after a messy break-up. At first, I had a lot of casual sex, but after a while I got bored of waking up with people I wasn't really that interested in. I decided to try Internet dating instead, and this led me to discover something I'd never tried before: cybersex.

It started when I 'met' James online. We got chatting when I got home from the pub one night. I'd got into the habit of checking my replies as soon as I got home because it sent me off to bed feeling good about myself. He'd sent me a really funny email and I replied there and then, not imagining he'd still be awake. He was, and we ended up pinging emails back and forth for about an hour. I'd been working my way through a bottle of wine during this time. When he suggested that we move on to an instant messaging programme, I was more than happy to agree, even though I'd never done it before – it would save the agonising wait in between emails.

I downloaded a messaging programme from a website he recommended, then logged in. He popped up instantly.

'Hi sexy.'
'Hi gorgeous.'
'So this is your first time messaging?'
'It is indeed.'
'Don't worry, I'll be gentle.'

The banter continued in similarly flirtatious tone and, before long, he'd said that he'd love to meet up. I made the mistake of asking what he'd like to do, and he – very charmingly – proceeded to tell me in excruciatingly sexy detail. I could feel myself getting wet and was drunk enough to tell him so. 'Why don't you do something about it?' was his sexy reply.

I'd never normally have done something like that but the conversation was really turning me on and I couldn't resist touching myself, all the while typing with the other hand to tell him what I was doing. This got him really hot and soon he was telling me that he was touching himself too. The more we chatted, the dirtier he got until I was confessing my filthiest fantasies. I ended up coming really hard, and he said he was coming shortly afterwards.

Since then, I've gone online most nights and we often talk for hours. The problem is that I've confessed so much about my desires that I'd be embarrassed for him to put a face to my name.

Lucinda, 36, dancer

Virtual fantasies

Another, more sophisticated, option is to live out your fantasies online in a virtual world. While this is undoubtedly safest if you just choose to indulge in cybersex with your existing partner, you can also extend your fantasy to include other people by getting involved in a MUD (Multi-User Dimension) experience which includes avatars (electronic representations of yourself) as well as virtual worlds to explore.

While most of these websites are by no means designed as a sexual tool, instead being a complete 'alternative world' existence, there are numerous sexual communities for adults only that form part of their 'universe', and were created so that people can share similar kinks and explore their fantasies together. No matter what your fantasy, you're likely to find people who'll want to 'play' with you, either individually or with both of you as a couple. Options go from online group sex, submission and domination to harder-core virtual activities such as vore (cannibalism as a fetish), age play (playing a character who's much older or younger than you really are) and furryism (assuming the role of an animal during sex). People involved in the group may not necessarily take part in any of these activities outside the virtual world (although some might); they're simply using the Internet as a way to share their fantasies with similarly minded people.

Virtual reality sex is obviously very different from the real thing as you can assume whatever persona you want to. If you've always liked the idea of being a blonde-haired, blue-eyed busty babe or a swarthy muscled man, all you need to do is create an 'avatar' that looks that way and your dreams will come true. You can assume a different gender from your own (including cross-gender), take on a different personality and generally test out different sides of your sexual persona, even if only for one night.

Of course, anyone you interact with could have done exactly the same thing, so you won't always know what you're getting. While this suspension of disbelief is one of the appeals of entering an online community, it does mean that you need to be careful. Never give away personal information, such as where you work, your address, your full name or your contact details. You should also be careful about which email address you use to sign in under as this will generally be visible to other people in the community (though it does vary depending on the platform you're using for your online romp). As such, it's best to create a separate email address that gives nothing away about your 'real' self.

When it comes to virtual sex, it's very easy to get carried away. If you decide to enter into this sort of play with your partner, you should set ground rules first, just as you would with a 'real' experience. Are you going to interact only with each other or are other people allowed to join in with what you're doing? Are you only going to play in the online world together or are you also likely to want to play with other people when you're alone? It may seem over-cautious but it's amazing how addictive cyber-sex can be, and there are numerous examples of people breaking up a real-life relationship to pursue an online affair. It's also worth mutually agreeing how much time you're going to allocate to virtual sex. It can be incredibly addictive and, unless you agree limits, you may find that one or both of you is indulging in online sex when the other would rather be talking, doing household chores together or having sex for real.

That said, as long as you agree guidelines with your partner before you start playing, and stick to them, virtual worlds can give you a new way to explore your fantasies together and provide you with fresh material to hone your erotic daydreams. Just make sure that your 'real world' activities don't get pushed back in favour of virtual play and you won't go far wrong.

TRUE CONFESSIONS
I CAME SECOND TO CANDY

When I first saw a magazine article about virtual worlds, I thought it looked like fun. My bloke Pete is a bit of a geek, so I suggested to him that we both created characters together and saw what it was like. I found it a bit tricky to use but when Pete bought some virtual money to help me tailor my look, I was really pleased. I tried to make his as realistic as possible, though I did improve his body a bit. He, on the other hand, asked if I minded having a sluttier character than I really am. We'd had a few glasses of wine and it seemed like a laugh; I've always had a bit of a naughty side, but I'm embarrassed about letting it show a lot of the time as it makes me feel a bit awkward the morning after. The idea of having an online persona that could be the wicked me seemed a perfect solution.

We decided to call her Candy as it sounds like a porn star's name, and set about creating her. I gave her bigger boobs than mine, and bought her some sexy but slightly trampy clothes from one of the stores.

After helping me get used to the way that the characters moved around the island, Pete suggested that he went into the spare room to use the laptop so that we could interact with each other purely as our characters. I agreed.

'You look sexy.'
'You helped create me.'
'I don't know what you mean.'

I realised then that he wanted to pretend we were strangers and decided that if I was really going to be Candy, that was probably the best idea. I added:

'Sorry. Was mixing you up with someone else.
You're pretty buff yourself.'
'Fancy going some place fun?'
'Sure.'

The next thing I knew, we were in a different location where avatars wearing sexy clothes were everywhere.

'This is a wild place, apparently,' Pete said. 'Wanna party?'

I went along with it, and as we walked around we saw avatars having sex all around us, man on man, woman on woman, orgies full of people – some with animal heads. It was wild, but because it wasn't real, I let bad Candy out. That night we ended up 'having sex' with another couple, and then Pete watched Candy with another woman (something we'd often talked about but I could never do in real life). After a couple of hours, Pete came through from the spare room, bent me over the sofa and had sex with me. Now, we often use cybersex as foreplay, and I'm really glad I saw that article.

Miranda, 28, beautician

Erotic writing

If you're too shy to interact with your partner about your fantasies 'live', even on the virtual plane, you may find it easier to write them an erotic story. You don't need to be a particularly great wordsmith to do this. Just write the way that you would talk to your partner and they'll be able to imagine you're in the room with them, whispering naughty thoughts in their ear.

You may choose to write a story that uses both of your names. Alternatively, if your fantasy is something that you're not 100 per cent convinced your partner will share, you can introduce distance by writing the story about a pair of 'strangers' meeting and getting it on in your fantasy scenario.

As a fun alternative that you can play together, you could write an erotic sentence, then pass the piece of paper to your partner so that they can follow your sentence up with one of their own. Take turns to write a sentence each and before too long, you'll have an erotic story that you've both created together. Then you can choose to make your fantasy come true, or simply ravage each other safe in the knowledge that you've already turned each other on.

EMILY'S EXPERIENCES: I'VE USED EROTICA TO SEDUCE

I've been writing erotica for about seven years, and I'd be lying if I said I've never used it to seduce someone. In fact, I've used it in numerous ways. After having flirtatious exchanges with one bloke for a long time and not 'sealing the deal', I sent him an erotic story with him in the starring role and got a date the next day, which went really rather well . . . I've written thinly veiled stories about encounters that I've had (with names changed, obviously) to stroke a lover's ego. And now I'm in a long-term relationship, I'll occasionally write my partner a short erotic story if I've been working hard all day, but want to give him a (not exactly subtle) hint that I'm in the mood and get him turned on all at once. Obviously, it helps that I write erotica for a living, but I've had several non-writers return the favour to me over the years and I've never been disappointed by the stories that have been written about me. There's something romantic about knowing someone's set aside a part of their day to think about what they want to do to you, rather than just going for the physical approach, and it's a gift that costs nothing other than time. More to the point, it often ends up with the erotic story coming true.

Enacting fantasies

Of course, there's nothing to say that you can't actually make your fantasy come true if it's suitable. Not every fantasy has to involve a cast of thousands or a complex role play. Sometimes the simplest things can work. If you fantasise about having sex in public, get into the car and drive somewhere suitably discreet (*see* Chapter Two for safety tips). Maybe there's a certain sex act that you've always been curious about but never tried, such as anal sex or using toys with each other. Or perhaps you like the idea of being thoroughly pampered before you have sex with your lover. Obviously, some fantasies require props or costumes, in which case role play will serve the purpose far better; others may be things that you wouldn't really like to happen, but find a turn-on as long as they stay purely in your mind. But if your fantasy is feasible, what's to stop you making it come true, as long as your partner is into the idea too (or willing to give it a try). As the song says, 'You've got to have a dream, if you don't have a dream, how you gonna make your dream come true?'

TRUE CONFESSIONS
DEEP IN THE COUNTRYSIDE

My girlfriend Carly is definitely a naughty minx. On our first date – if you can call meeting in a bar a date – she dragged me into the toilets after we'd been chatting for about ten minutes and gave me the best blow job I'd ever had then walked out without a word to join her mates again. She didn't even offer me her number, and I had to wait until she'd finished chatting before I could ask her for it. On our second date, she asked me to have anal sex with her. I'd never done it before but was more than happy to oblige. Afterwards she asked me about my fantasies and I told her that I'd always liked the idea of al fresco action. We didn't really discuss it (we got distracted), but the next time I saw her she turned up wearing a long coat and told me that she was taking me for a drive. Seeing the look in her eyes, I wasn't going to argue.

She drove into a nearby forest, parked her car in a lay-by and beckoned me to follow her through a gap in the trees. Once we were far away enough from the road she dropped her coat to reveal that she was naked underneath. Then she lay down on her coat and beckoned me over. I didn't need asking twice and was inside her in seconds. It didn't last long. The feeling of the wind against my skin, the thought that anyone could catch us at it and the sheer nerve that she had to get naked in the open turned me on so much that I couldn't hold back. The reality was even better than the fantasy – it felt like I was doing something that I shouldn't – and when she made me go down on her after I'd come, it was beyond my wildest daydreams. She was so unselfconscious and that was one of the sexiest things ever to me.

That was three years ago. I'm still with Carly, and we still have sex outdoors to this day, but I'll always remember that first time particularly fondly because it was such a surprise and showed me exactly how wild she could be.

Greg, 32, caterer

Role play

Possibly the most explicit of all the fantasy games you can play, role play involves getting dressed up in the relevant costumes and actually pretending to be whatever your fantasy entails, whether that's a fireman and grateful rescued woman or, at the more extreme end of things, a giant furry badger and a giant furry panda (yes, really – it's known as furryism). You can also use scripts, different locations and props. While role play does require a bit of effort, it's a fun way to help both of you really immerse yourselves in your fantasy situation by making each other's ultimate fantasy lover 'exist'.

TRUE CONFESSIONS
MY BIRTHDAY ROLE PLAY WAS A PRIVATE DANCER

For my last birthday, I told my girlfriend that I wanted a surprise. On the day, I got a text message from her telling me to meet her at her flat at 8 p.m. I turned up, expecting her to have made a nice dinner, but was amazed when she opened the door wearing a corset, stockings, heels and a thong. She's usually a bit of a tomboy, so seeing her with her hair done and make-up on was a bit of a shock. She led me through to the front room and I saw a pole in the middle of the room.

'Sit down,' she said, thrusting a pile of Monopoly money into my hands. I did as I was told, she gave me a beer, then pressed play on the stereo. She started dancing around the pole and I could feel myself getting hard as she showed off her beautiful body. As the first song finished, she spun around the pole and I applauded, but it wasn't over. She came over to where I was sitting and started to give me a lap dance, rubbing herself against me on my lap then grinding away. I almost came there and then but I think she knew how much she was turning me on because she moved away then bent over and whispered in my ear, 'The management here will turn a blind eye if you give me enough money.'

I handed the pile of Monopoly money over to her and she started to strip, still rubbing up against me, then undid my fly, dropped to her knees and started to give me a blow job. Just as I was about to come, she pulled away.

'You can have anything you want,' she said.

I was going to ask her to continue what she'd been doing, but then she pulled a bottle of lube and some condoms from behind my chair, bent over with her legs straight in front of me and ran her fingers between her legs, before parting her cheeks for me. I realised what she meant. I'd been asking her if we could try anal sex for a while and she'd clearly decided to give it to me for my birthday.

I pulled my clothes off, then pushed her on to the floor on all fours and slathered her in lubricant, fingering her until she was moaning in pleasure. It didn't take me long to come: the sight of her in those sexy stockings, and the feel of doing something so taboo with my 'naughty stripper' girlfriend was too much for me. It was my best ever birthday.

Simon, 24, IT manager

'Remember to keep it fun. The hint is in the title role PLAY.'

Mistress Absolute, professional Dominatrix

Know the Risks

While fantasy and role play are among the safest kinky things to try, there are still risks to be aware of before you start playing. Some of these are practical and others are more emotional.

However, all are easily navigable as long as you go about things in the right way.

The biggest mistake that people are inclined to make when playing with fantasy is to become over-reliant on it. While it's all very well playing 'Highwayman and Wanton Wench' once a week or so, if you do it every time you get intimate you may end up feeling that you're in just as much of a rut as if you only ever have sex in the missionary position with the lights off. You may also find that it's harder to get aroused without incorporating fantasy if you use it every time you make love.

There's also the risk that your image of your fantasy may be so refined that you are disappointed if it doesn't go exactly as you've envisaged it should you choose to live it out. The key to having a fun fantasy experience is to go with the flow.

TIPS FROM THE SCENE

Avoid perfectionism. The easiest way to start into role play – after all the talking and discussion and negotiation are done – is to plan the start of the scene, and then let it run its course. If Little Red Riding Hood is tripping through the forest and the big bad wolf jumps out from behind a tree and ties her to the aforementioned tree, you are on your way. Trying to play a fantasy start to finish with every detail just the way it is in your mind when you rock yourself to sleep at night is basically too much to ask. You are exploring roles and sex; a spirit of, 'Let's see where this goes', is the best place to start.

Dossie Easton, sexpert and author of *Radical Ecstasy*

Certain fantasies may reinforce negative feelings or beliefs. For example, if you fantasise about an ex-partner, it's liable to take longer for you to get over them; and if your partner doesn't share your fantasies but you insist on incorporating them into your sex life anyway, it can drive a wedge between you.

In the book *Private Thoughts: Exploring the Power of Women's Sexual Fantasies*, Wendy Maltz and Suzie Boss provide a list of questions to ask yourself to help you evaluate whether a fantasy is healthy or problematic:

- Does the fantasy lead to risky or dangerous behaviour?

- Does the fantasy feel out of control or compulsive?

- Is the content of the fantasy disturbing or repulsive?

- Does the fantasy hinder recovery or personal growth?

- Does the fantasy lower my self-esteem or block self-acceptance?

- Does the fantasy distance me from my real-life partner?

- Does the fantasy harm my intimate partner or anyone else?

- Does the fantasy cause sexual problems?

- Does the fantasy really belong to someone else?

If you answer 'Yes' to one or more of these questions, it's worth examining whether the fantasy in question is actually enhancing your sex life or would be better off relegated into the past.

If need be, you can always seek counselling to help you figure out why you're drawn to something that's damaging.

That said, if you keep them to youself, you can have entirely healthy fantasies that other people may find disturbing but don't do you any harm whatsoever, so don't think that you have to moderate your fantasies to fit in with other people's moral standards. Just make sure that you understand the effect that your fantasies have on you: and if that's nothing more than getting you aroused in super-quick time, carry on with your salacious daydreams.

And then there's the practical side of things. If you're having phone sex you need to make sure that you trust your partner not to record it to play to their mates, and that there's no one around to overhear your not-so-sweet nothings. If you live in a shared house and have a phone extension, unplug it before you start your call – the last thing you want is a flatmate (or worse, family member) listening in on what you're saying and teasing you about it for ever.

Similarly, with cybersex and virtual worlds, make sure that you delete your conversation log after you finish chatting, unless you want a red face the next time you take your computer in to be repaired or let someone use your computer and they inadvertently open the wrong file. If you want to keep the transcripts to refer back to at a later date, save them into a separate folder and lock it. It may seem overcautious, but given the level of intimacy you're likely to share with your partner, you probably won't want to risk anyone else discovering what you've said.

The same goes with erotic writing, albeit to a lesser extent as you can pretend that you were writing it in the hope of getting it published. However, if you want to email your partner an erotic story at work, it's probably better to upload it to a website like Cliterati.co.uk or Literotica.com then send them the link, rather than just pasting it into the email or sending it as an attachment. That way, if anyone does discover it, they'll just think you're sending your lover a random smutty story that they might enjoy, rather than sharing your own thoughts about what you'd like to do with them, a vibrator and a pot of strawberry jam. It also makes it less identifiable should your partner pass the story on to anyone else, as you can use a pseudonym or post your story anonymously so that your identity remains hidden.

Role play involves, potentially, the most risks, as it covers such a wide range of possibilities. While some role-play games, such as 'Prince Charming and Sleeping Beauty', may be mild enough that you don't need to set any limits beforehand, if there's any element of power play involved, in which one of you is dominant and the other submissive, you need to make sure that you agree limits before you start, and that you have a 'safe word'. This is a word that you wouldn't usually use when you're having sex that means, 'Stop right now'. You could pick a word like 'pineapple' or 'armadillo', but if that seems too comedic and unsexy, opt for the traffic-light system in which red means, 'Stop immediately', amber means, 'Tone it down' and green means, 'Carry on, all is well'. This system has the advantage of being common on the fetish scene which means that people will understand what you're saying should you decide that you want to play at a fetish party. But by far the best safe word is solid communication. As long as you've discussed everything thoroughly with your partner before you start, you should find that you don't need to use your safe word very often at all, as you already know what your partner does and doesn't like.

Another possible pitfall is that you may find that certain role plays bring out sides of your character that you don't like, or give you flashbacks to negative experiences. If this happens, take a break, tell your partner your reasons for doing so and think about why your role play has had this effect on you. There's no reason that such experiences need be entirely negative: expressing things can help you to work them through, after all. However, you should never force yourself to carry on doing something that makes you feel uncomfortable, even if your partner is at the point of orgasm. You can always resume sexual activity once you feel better, whether that is the following day or week.

As a general rule, it's unlikely that you'll run into trouble experimenting with fantasy and role play, as long as you stick to the ground rules. We spend a lot of time playing as kids; exploring fantasy and role play is simply a more adult way of playing games.

TIPS FROM THE SCENE

Remember, there are some fantasies that are best kept as exactly that. It's amazing what unforeseen emotions pop up when you start acting things out. I was once seeing a submissive woman, Emma, and her master, Andrew. Emma was desperate to act out a particular fantasy: Andrew had a human-size cage and she wanted to be locked in it, naked, and placed at the foot of his bed so she had to sit and watch while he and I had sex. It all sounded pretty good to me, but there was a slight hitch. While Emma was quite happy to be put in the cage when just Andrew was in the room, as soon as I arrived she started crying and had to be released and comforted. She wouldn't admit it at the time, but the fantasy, while great in her head, triggered too many scary feelings of jealousy and insecurity once it started to happen for real. We never did get round to doing that one. Dammit.

Goldie, 28, submissive

Accessories

Fantasy and role play can both be aided with a host of accessories, whether purely mental or more physical in nature. Certain books, videos and websites can fuel the fire of your fantasies, while investing in some sexy outfits or props can add extra reality to your fantasy life, if that's what you want to do. For more specific recommendations on books, websites and films that you may find useful or appealing, *see* Resources, p. 269.

Erotic books

Erotic stories have existed for hundreds of years and are a wonderful way to access your existing fantasies and find new ones. Unless you have a firmly defined view of what your fantasies entail, it makes sense to spend your money on erotica anthologies, rather than books on a particular theme. This gives you greater scope to explore your fantasies with your partner and find things that turn both of you on. An erotic anthology is also the gift that keeps on giving if you pick something that you think will turn your partner on.

Erotic books can be used in various ways. You can read your partner a sexy bedtime story and see if it works as foreplay; you can suggest that your lover read an erotic story while you finish work, then call when they need you; or you can bookmark certain pages or scenes with Post-it notes reading, for example, 'Fancy trying this?' You can give erotic books as birthday and Christmas presents, so that you've constantly got fresh inspiration for your sex life, or buy them for yourself if you feel that your fantasies are getting a little worn out.

If you're not a big fan of reading, you can also buy erotica anthologies in audio format to listen to on your computer or iPod. Listening to an erotic story on your way home after a hard day at work can be a good way to de-stress and get yourself in the mood for your partner. And it's even more thrilling knowing that nobody else around you on public transport will have a clue about what you're listening to, so it'll be your own erotic secret.

Sexy films

Again, the DVD market is saturated with material that can help you hone your fantasies. One of the easiest ways for you and your partner to navigate this market is to visit a site that streams videos on demand on your computer. These sites allow you to peruse a huge database of material and determine what turns both of you on. If you don't have Internet access, there are numerous couple-friendly sex shops around nowadays, particularly in major cities.

The selection of films available has come a long way from the days of moustachioed men humping orange women to cries of 'Mein Gott!' Films with female directors are often more couple-friendly (see Resources, p. 269 for recommendations), but an increasing number of male producers are now also realising that unless their films appeal to both men and women, they're missing out on a major part of the market.

Some people, particularly women, have issues with watching pornography, fearing that they'll be negatively compared to the stars of the film. This isn't something to be concerned about, not least because the men in porn films nowadays tend to be buff studs with eight-inch-plus cocks, so your man has just as much to feel insecure about as you do. Watching a porn film together isn't about comparing what you've got to what you could have. It's about getting inspiration for future fantasies together, sharing a sexy evening with your lover and, to be blunt, getting easy mutual foreplay. Who knows, it could even inspire you to make your own home movie as a very personal pleasure.

Outfits and props

Most sex shops sell a variety of kinky outfits, from sexy plumber to naughty nurse, Playboy bunny to army officer.

Alternatively, you can make your own outfits from your existing wardrobe. For example, with a little imagination and a little black dress you can be turned into:

- a French maid, if you add a frilly apron, cute white lace hat and a feather duster

- a Dominatrix, if you add a whip, high boots and a pair of handcuffs

- a stripper, if you add long gloves and jewellery.

Or, with a pair of combat trousers, you can become:

- a plumber, with the addition of a tool belt

- an army officer, with the addition of a tight T-shirt and maybe a toy gun

- a burglar, with the addition of a stocking over the head!

TIPS FROM THE SCENE

Thrift stores are great for costume collections; sometimes I am amazed at how much sexy lingerie I find. I imagine hopeful spouses everywhere shopping at Victoria's Secret for anniversary presents that wind up in the bag for the charity store.

Dossie Easton, sexpert and author of *Radical Ecstasy*

(**Note:** it should go without saying, but if you do buy lingerie from a charity shop, make sure you wash it thoroughly before you wear it. It's entirely possible to find unused undies if you hunt around enough too.)

Toy stores are a surprisingly useful place to go to ramp up your fantasy collection. A toy stethoscope will add realism to a game of doctors and nurses, a pair of horns can turn you into an evil devil girl and a plastic knife can be used in burglar fantasies.

With a little imagination, almost anything can be turned into kinky attire, so just let your mind wander and see how sexy you can get.

Are You Ready For More?

So, now you've dipped your toe in the water of fetish and, with any luck, discovered it's not as murky as you may, at first, have suspected. Once you have an idea of your fantasies, you can either leave it there, safe in the knowledge that you're now a little more self-aware, share your erotic thoughts with your partner to help you develop a greater bond or tread further along the path of fetish and explore more of the wonders that kinky sex has to offer. You are the only person who can decide what your sexual future holds, and as long as you make sure that you abide by what you've learned so far, you'll be fine. But if you do want to delve a little deeper, grab my hand. I promise I won't look at what you're doing. Or maybe I will – if you want me to – because we're about to enter the world of voyeurism and exhibitionism: an eye-opening experience if ever there was one . . .

CHAPTER TWO

Voyeurism and Exhibitionism

Once you've opened the door to your fantasies, there's a whole host of kinks that you may find lurking inside your mind, and voyeurism and exhibitionism are two of the most common. The former involves looking at people naked or engaged in sexual acts, while the latter applies to people getting horny from showing off their own naked form.

While voyeurism is technically classified as a paraphilia (or sexual deviation) if a person *needs* to observe others who are naked or engaged in sexual acts in order to become aroused, most people get turned on to some degree when observing other people's nudity or catching others in flagrante. Indeed, the entire porn industry is based on exactly that premise, and if everyone who watched an X-rated movie headed to the GP to cure their 'compulsion', the doctors' surgeries would be more overstretched than they already are.

The common stereotype is that men are visually aroused whereas women require more of a cerebral approach. It's certainly true that there's no evolutionary advantage to women getting aroused from merely looking at a bloke naked (though it would make the whole mating thing a lot more pleasant for everyone concerned), whereas for a man an ability to attain an erection on first sight increases his chances of being able to propagate the species. As such, this theory does make sense on a superficial level. However, research shows that women get just as physically aroused as men do when watching footage of naked people, and, as society deems female sexuality more acceptable, women are increasingly amassing porn collections, surfing the Internet for smut and buying magazines that feature men (and women) in a state of undress. Indeed, when we first launched *Scarlet* magazine, a UK-based sex magazine for women, the biggest complaint that we got was that there weren't enough pictures of blokes with their kit off (and it's still the biggest complaint to this day, no matter how much male totty we add).

Sadly, the archaic attitudes surrounding porn in the UK mean that magazines have to adhere to the Mull of Kintyre guideline which states that a man's penis may not be shown if it is more erect than the angle at which the Mull of Kintyre sticks out from Scotland (look it up on a map – at best it's an unimpressive semi-flaccid member), and showing pictures of men with flaccid members hardly compares to the thousands of magazines out there showing women with erect nipples and spread, glistening lips. But there is no question that women enjoy looking at images of sexy men with hard cocks, and the Internet has proved that if you build it, they will certainly come . . .

And it's not just British women who like looking at a man in a state of undress. America has some of the best female-friendly porn sites around, and in Italy professional women are among the highest consumers of pay-per-view porn. Female directors such as Candida Royalle, Anna Span and Petra Joy all have hot, hardcore and couple-friendly films available throughout the world, and I've had endless letters over the years from women asking where they can find the best gay porn for girlie nights in spent leching over buff young men with impressive members (getting off with other buff young men with impressive members; well, as men discovered years ago, same-sex action gives you twice the amount of hotness to look at).

Of course, it hardly needs saying that a lot of men quite like watching porn too.

Looking at other people naked and/or engaging in sexual acts gives us the chance not only to get turned on, but also to assess other people's bodies and see how 'normal' we are by comparison. The quest to be 'normal' is a constant part of being human, so it's an easy way to get reassurance. And you thought that you were a pervert just for covertly checking out your friend in the shower at the gym.

The other side of the observational coin is exhibitionism. Just as voyeurs love the idea of looking at people who are naked or in sexual situations, exhibitionists get a kick out of showing off their own bodies. Blessed is the relationship that comprises one voyeur and one exhibitionist.

Luckily, exhibitionism is another kink that most people find arousing at the milder levels, so it shouldn't be hard to find someone to indulge your fetish. Many women have fantasies about being a stripper for a baying horde of men and, even at the tamest end of the scale, research shows that about a quarter of people find sex extra arousing when their partner looks at their face during orgasm – surely the most 'naked' anyone can be with someone else. Gazing at your partner during sex is a key part of tantra and has long been associated with Eastern erotic techniques, which just goes to show that sometimes the oldest advice is the best.

Masturbating in front of a partner is also incredibly common, with about half of men and women putting on a sex show for their lover on occasion. Not only does this give your partner an arousing visual treat, it also shows them how you like to be touched, so it's a useful learning tool as well as a bit of kinky fun.

TRUE CONFESSIONS
WE MASTURBATE TOGETHER

One of my favourite things is playing with myself in front of my husband. I grew up being told that touching yourself 'down there' was dirty, and even though I know that's rubbish nowadays, I like the idea of doing something 'forbidden' while he watches me, particularly if he pretends that he's caught me in the act and is punishing me by making me carry on, even though I find it humiliating.

Sometimes I just use my fingers but recently, he's started giving me toys to use when he 'catches' me and ordering me to put on a sex show for him. There's something about having his gaze on me that makes me feel much hornier than I do purely through masturbation alone.

Sometimes he masturbates while he watches me, which I find incredibly sexy. At other times, he'll wait until I'm just about to come then pull my hand or the toy away and slide into me. Either way is fine by me! Even when my husband's not in the house, I often close my eyes and imagine that he's watching me when I'm masturbating because it gives everything an extra frisson.

Linda, 36, teacher

And then there are people who take it that little bit further: according to Queendom.com, about 7 per cent of people have had someone walk in on them during sex and found it a turn-on (and that's not even taking into account all those who wish that that had happened to them). Public sex is a taboo act and taboos often act as sexual triggers – after all, it can be fun doing something that's 'naughty' – so it's hardly surprising that getting caught in the act can be a turn-on for some.

When it comes down to it, being gazed at adoringly by someone who finds you sexually attractive is a great ego boost, so it's hardly surprising that, for many people, showing their body off provides a sexual thrill. And as long as it's done in a safe, sane and consensual way there's nothing wrong with that at all.

Know the Risks

When it comes to living out voyeuristic or exhibitionistic fantasies, you need to be well aware of your local laws as well as applying common sense and following the guidelines below. While some countries and states have a relaxed attitude towards public nudity, others find it incredibly offensive and you could find yourself spending time in jail for indulging your kink (just look at what happened to the couple who got it on publicly in Dubai). As such, it's always best to play it safe unless you know exactly what penalties you might face.

It should go without saying that any voyeuristic activity should take place only with consenting partners. Looking at someone in a state of undress or engaged in a sexual act without their consent is breaching their personal space. Instead, stick to role plays with your partner or nights out at fetish clubs where everyone is more than happy to be ogled.

Conversely, you should only indulge in exhibitionistic behaviour with willing partners or parties. No matter how great your body is, there's no guarantee that everyone wants to see it and flashing or streaking in front of people who may be offended just isn't on. Get down to a nudist beach if you want to feel the wind on your skin. At least everyone knows what to expect there.

But by far the best way to enjoy voyeuristic and exhibitionistic fantasies is with your partner. After all, beauty is in the eye of the beholder and someone who loves you is likely to see you as very beautiful indeed. While you're enjoying the thrill of being watched, they'll be getting off on seeing your naked form and vice versa. And the more time you spend with each other naked, the more confident you'll become about your body, which can only be good for your relationship.

Share the Love

If you have exhibitionistic or voyeuristic urges, don't be afraid to share them with your partner. However, as with sharing your fantasies, it's best to stick to the milder end of the spectrum, at least until you've established whether your partner shares your desires. Don't just grab your lover by the genitals when you're at a party and demand that they do you right there, right then. If you fantasise about being watched during sex, tell your partner that you feel frisky at the idea of leaving the curtains open while you're at it so that anyone can see what you're doing. And if you like the idea of watching other people have sex, start by selecting and watching some porn together rather than trying to drag your lover off to a swinging party or peep-show booth. Only work up to more flagrant acts if and when you and your partner both feel comfortable with the idea. You can also choose from one of the games below as a mild way to explore your fetishistic desires.

Here's Looking at You: Games for Voyeurs

There are numerous ways to give a lover a voyeuristic thrill, whether by being the object of their desire or by letting go of a little jealousy and joining them while they ogle someone else altogether. Although the latter can be a lot of fun, it's only advisable if it won't create any relationship conflict. While some couples have no problem with their partner looking at other men or women in a naked or sexual situation, say at a strip club or in an adult film (some people with really low jealousy levels can even go as far as to observe their partner with another lover), others find the idea appalling. Only you know your boundaries so make sure that you and your partner discuss these thoroughly before you initiate any games.

Once you've established your comfort levels, choose from one of the following options:

Striptease

Visiting striptease clubs offers the chance of a voyeuristic thrill without any risk of getting arrested. Although such clubs are traditionally perceived as the bastion of men, the gender imbalance is less pronounced than you might expect, particularly among people who only visit such places on occasion. According to Queendom.com, 32 per cent of women go to strip clubs once or twice per year, compared to 43 per cent of men. And then there's the rise of burlesque clubs to take into account: one look around the room should be enough to tell you that lots of women enjoy watching striptease just as much as men do. And while the majority of men say they prefer strip clubs with only female dancers, just 20 per cent of women insist on having male strippers around in order to find strip clubs a turn-on, which goes to show it's not only men who can appreciate the female form in a sexual way.

Going to a strip club with a partner has a very different dynamic from going alone, offering a host more opportunities than merely observing someone take their clothes off. You may choose to buy your partner a dance and surreptitiously grope them under the table once the dancer has finished. You could both wear remote-controlled sex toys and give your partner a buzz under their clothes while they watch the dancers, without anyone else realising what you're doing. Or you could even both have a dance at the same time. However, do be warned that drinks in strip clubs tend to be extortionately priced, and if you go to a club on a quiet night you'll be bombarded with women all eager to dance for you which can sometimes feel a bit too 'hard sell' to be sexy. It's also worth checking whether the club is couple-friendly. While the majority of them are nowadays, you don't want to get into a situation where one or both of you feels out of place.

Sadly, there are very few good male strip bars around outside the gay market so this experience is best if the woman is bicurious or likes the idea of seeing her partner with another woman. That said, you could always hire a male escort to do a striptease for you both in the privacy of your own home, should you so wish.

Whichever option you go for, do be aware that one or both of you might get jealous and don't dabble if you think it's likely to cause relationship problems. However, with an open mind there's no reason why you shouldn't both have a fun evening – and it will probably get even more entertaining once you're home . . .

TRUE CONFESSIONS
ANOTHER WOMAN MADE MY MAN HORNY –
AND I DIDN'T MIND

One of the hottest nights of my life came about because my man and I went to a lap-dancing club together after I'd read about the idea in a magazine. We ordered our drinks and snuggled up with each other. I put my hand protectively on his knee when a stripper approached, but when she asked if it was OK to sit with us she gestured to the seat next to me rather than my man, so I soon relaxed.

After introducing herself as Mercedes, she started making polite conversation. She had big brown eyes and, even though I'd never really fancied a woman before, there was something about her that I found sexy, so when she asked if we wanted a dance, I shot my man a look as he started to decline and asked how much it would cost for me to buy him one. He looked shocked but was happy to acquiesce.

If you'd have asked me before that night if I'd have wanted to see my man with another woman, I'd have been horrified, but watching Mercedes push his legs apart then lean over him and swing her long hair back and forth over his chest as she pushed her dress down over her body was strangely hot. She danced around in her under-wear for a while then unclipped her bra. She took her time though, only pulling her bra off once she'd turned around to wave her bum in his face, meaning that I got to see her breasts before he did – and I was impressed. They were slightly larger than mine with stiff, brown nipples and a fullness that made me want to touch them.

She sat back on my man's lap and began to grind against him. I could tell he was getting aroused, which was hardly surprising given that she was only wearing a G-string and seemed to be pushing her buttocks deeper into his lap with every move. When the song came to an end, she stood up, kissed him on the cheek and asked if he'd enjoyed it. He nodded his head, seemingly incapable of speech. Before I knew what I was doing, I found myself saying, 'I'd like a dance too, if you're OK dancing for women?' My man looked shocked, but didn't stop me when she said she was more than happy to dance for me and I thrust more notes into her hand.

She seemed to dance more slowly for me. I could smell her sweet scent as she brushed her hair over my breasts, which were quite well revealed in my low-cut top. I could feel my nipples stiffening and when she leaned forward and whispered, 'You're sexy,' in my ear, I felt a rush of juices between my legs. She performed a similar routine for me as she had for my man but when it came to the lap-dancing part, instead of sitting down, she straddled my lap with one of her thighs between my legs so that I could feel the friction. I sat there, helpless, as she reduced me to putty. She kissed me on the cheek at the end of my song too, and I was left sitting there with my man, both of us feeling horny as hell. Needless to say we had great sex that night.

Casey, 28, web designer

Mirror, mirror

One of the mildest forms of voyeurism is having sex in front of the mirror (or simply contorting yourself so that you can get a better view of proceedings) and it's a hugely popular kink: 72 per cent of women and 88 per cent of men like watching the penis enter the vagina. As such, incorporating a mirror into a sex session is a good way to cater to voyeuristic and exhibition-istic desires.

It's worth spending some time positioning the mirror before you have sex. It can be very frustrating if you get down to it, only to realise that your partner's leg is blocking the view, or that you need to crane your neck uncomfortably in order to see anything other than your man's swinging testicles. To avoid this, get into position fully clothed or wearing lingerie, and simulate sex to check that you can both see as much as you want to. You might get the urge to giggle, but if you do, there's no need to hold it back. Laughing with (though never at) your partner during sex is a great way to strengthen the bond between you and it relaxes you which will boost your libido too.

Depending on the view that you're after, you may choose to have the mirror to the side of the bed, at the end of the bed or even stuck to the ceiling. (**Note**: do not attempt the third option unless you have the right equipment. Having a mirror fall on your head midway through the proceedings will do nothing to enhance the mood.) Chat to your partner before-hand about their expectations and the kind of view that they'd like too. It may be that with a little helpful parting of cheeks or spreading of thighs you'll both be able to see things in graphic-ally hot detail. Conversely, it may be that they don't really want to see right up your bum when you're having sex, so be aware of your positioning if this is the case.

Once you've found the perfect position to observe your-selves in the mirror, lay out any toys, condoms, lubricant and whatever else you like to use during sex near to where you'll be getting it on. You don't want the distraction of getting out of position once you've started, so having everything close to hand will make things go a lot more smoothly.

And if you're going to the effort of having sex in front of a mirror, it's also worth spending a little time on making sure you look as good as possible beforehand. Trim any errant back hair, tidy those pubes, slip into your sexiest undies (that goes for men as well as women) and make yourself as sexy as possible. After all, you're going to be starring in a private sex show just for the two of you: make sure it's the best show in town.

TRUE CONFESSIONS
MIRRORS MADE OUR NIGHT

My man and I decided to have a dirty weekend at a posh hotel. After a lovely dinner, we got into bed and snuggled up. I was feeling really affectionate towards Shane as the day had gone really well. Then he whispered in my ear, 'God, that brings back memories,' and pointed to the mirrored wardrobe at the end of the bed. It reflected the whole of the bed and both of us.

'Go on . . .' I said.

'Well, when I was a teenager, I had a wardrobe like that in my room and used to watch myself having sex all the time. Half the girls didn't even notice.'

'That's terrible,' I laughed, but felt a bit of a thrill at the idea.

Shane started nibbling my neck which always gets me going. At first I batted him away but he's so good that soon I was burying my head in the pillow so that I didn't moan and wake up the people next door. He pushed my big T-shirt up and started kissing down my body.

'Look at how beautiful you are,' he said.

I looked in the mirror and, in the dim light, I did think I looked pretty sexy. There was no sign of my cellulite and I liked the contrast of his tanned skin against my pale skin. He started to suck on my nipples, and I loved the way I could see them stiffen. As he got lower and lower down, I found myself being more drawn to the lewd sight in the mirror and didn't even want to blink in case I missed something: I loved the way that I could see his pert bum reflected as he licked me, and it was hot seeing my back arch as he got me more and more turned on.

We ended up having sex in front of the mirror, although I did make him cover my mouth with his hand because I was so horny. It was over pretty quickly because we were both so turned on, but I still remember it as one of the sexiest nights we've ever had. Needless to say, when we got home, we bought a big mirror for our bedroom (although I did draw the line when Shane suggested we got a mirror on the ceiling)!

Kirsty, 27, chiropractor

Narcissus revisited

You don't have to have a partner involved to enjoy a voyeuristic session. Ever since Narcissus first turned into the well-known flower for staring at his reflection in adoration of his own beauty, it's been known that some people enjoy self-indulgently admiring their own image and this is just as true when it comes to sex. Queendom.com found 23 per cent and 28 per cent of men have masturbated in front of the mirror once, while a self-loving 3 per cent of women and 5 per cent of men always do. So, even when you're all alone, there are plenty of opportunities to get kinky.

If you like the idea of incorporating some voyeurism into your self-love sessions, start by making sure that you have the house to yourself (unless, of course, you have exhibitionistic desires – and willing watchers – too). Pamper yourself with a long bath and groom yourself to perfection, whether through shaving or trimming your pubic hair, manicuring your nails or exfoliating your body until it glows. If you're going to spend time adoring yourself in the mirror, you may as well make the view as good as it can possibly be.

Once you've finished bathing, get dressed up in the underwear or whatever outfit that makes you feel sexiest (if you're male, a pair of tight Calvins is almost always flattering). If you look your best, your confidence will only grow the more you look at yourself, and you can always gradually peel said outfit off in front of the mirror as you get more turned on. Perfect your appearance with any finishing touches like make-up, eyebrow plucking or rubbing oil into your skin to define your muscles, then settle yourself down in front of a mirror and seduce yourself. Look yourself in the eyes. Admire your face, your chest, your legs. Run your hand over your body and look at the way that it responds, whether that's the stiffening of your nipples or a rush of blood to your chest or lower down. Slip your underwear off and look at your genitals before you touch them. Think sexy thoughts or just admire the view and watch how your genitals change as they get more engorged with blood. Imagine that you are seeing yourself through a stranger's eyes: what would you particularly admire about yourself? Ignore any flaws you might perceive yourself to have; you can guarantee that a lover wouldn't notice them because they'd feel so aroused that you'd got naked for them. Only touch yourself when you can't hold back any longer. You may want to squint to better imagine that you're watching someone else or you might revel in the fact that you're watching yourself get turned on.

Masturbating in front of a mirror won't just provide you with a voyeuristic kick – it can also help boost your self-esteem, particularly if you look yourself in the eyes while you're doing it. You're accepting that you're worthy of self-love in one of the most basic ways: by loving yourself!

TRUE CONFESSIONS
I LOVE MYSELF

Ever since I first started masturbating, I've had a ritual around it which I'm guessing some people might find a bit weird and kinky. I make a real effort to get dressed up, with false eyelashes, lots of burlesque style make-up, nipple tassels, a corset, stockings and suspenders, boa and high-heeled shoes. While I'm getting dressed I can feel my excitement building; I sometimes pinch my nipples or pull my hair as I'm getting ready, but I don't touch myself anywhere else because the anticipation is one of the main things that turns me on.

Once I'm ready, which usually takes at least an hour, I can already feel myself wet underneath my frilly knickers but I still make myself wait. I pour myself a glass of wine and watch myself in the mirror as I slowly sip it. Only then do I put my favourite sexy song on – an old Pearl

Bailey recording – and start to strip for myself. I look myself in the eye as I take my clothes off, and tease myself with my feather boa and blow kisses at myself. I imagine that I'm in the audience watching myself perform rather than seeing myself in a mirror, and I gyrate for myself, knowing how much it's turning the 'me' in the audience on.

By the time the song comes to the end, I'm left wearing nothing but my stockings, suspenders, heels and nipple tassels. At this point, I spread my legs and watch my fingers darting in and out of my pussy as I make myself come. I always use my hands. I tried using a toy for a while but I came too quickly and it wasn't as intense without a long build-up.

It might sound like a hassle, and I'd be lying if I said I always masturbate in this way because sometimes I don't have the time, but I always have the best orgasms when I go through this ritual. I guess it helps that I'm bisexual as it means I can imagine my breasts belong to another woman if I start to lose momentum from staring at myself. I'd never tell a partner about my secret. One of my exes did catch me in the act but luckily it was early enough in my 'routine' that I could pretend I was practising and he believed me. But I don't feel ashamed of it really. It's just something that is part of me.

Flora, 35, burlesque performer

Show and tell

Of course, masturbation isn't something you need to save purely for yourself. If you and your partner both have voyeuristic desires, you're an exhibitionist to their voyeur or you simply fancy trying something a little bit different, then masturbating in front of each other can be a fantastic experience.

As with masturbating for yourself, make an effort to ensure you look as good as possible. You may even choose to incorporate a fantasy element, imagining that you're a high-class escort who's been paid to perform for a rich client, or you're working in a seedy peep-show booth and have to do anything your audience requests. If you opt for a fantasy scenario, share it with your partner so that you can both click into character – assuming, of course, that they like the idea too.

You might want to masturbate purely manually or you may want to use toys. Again, it's worth discussing this before you start to play: the last thing you want is to pull out a maxi vibro-dong, only to watch your partner pale and shrivel when they see 'the competition', or to slip a masturbation sheath over your member only to see your lover collapse in giggles.

Even though you're putting on a show for your partner, don't feel obliged to masturbate in a 'porn film' way. It's infinitely better to show your partner the way that you actually touch yourself when you're alone than to put on an elaborate performance that leaves you cold. Genuine arousal is so much hotter to watch than faked gyrations; not to mention that your partner will only learn what you like if you show them what you really do.

Conversely, while you're watching, act naturally. If what you see turns you on, don't be afraid to start masturbating as well. It's a great compliment to your partner and will probably speed their climax.

Once you've climaxed, you have various options. You can sit back and watch your partner masturbate, move on to touching your partner or simply curl up in each other's arms and enjoy the afterglow.

TRUE CONFESSIONS
MUTUAL MASTURBATION IS MY FAVOURITE THING

I've been single and playing the field for the last couple of years. At first, I leaped into bed with anyone on the first night because I was making up for lost time after being stuck in a relationship rut. However, I soon discovered that this meant I was working my way through everyone at my local club night far too quickly and I needed to slow down or I'd run out of men. That's when I decided to go for mutual masturbation instead: the way I figured it, both parties get to have an orgasm but the guy will still come back for more because he hasn't actually had sex. Or at least that was my initial reasoning.

But after I did it for the first time, I found it such a turn-on that I wanted it more than sex! There's something sexy about seeing a man touching himself, seeing his hand slide up and down a hard cock, and knowing that he's holding back from having sex because he's been told that he can't have it. I've got quite into taunting men while they masturbate too, saying things like, 'Would you like to be inside me?' and, 'I bet you'd love to taste me.' It's amazing how much it turns men on; I guess they like being denied, even though they're the ones constantly begging for sex. Or perhaps I've just had sex with perverts.

Elizabeth, 28, shop assistant

Hide and seek

To add a kinkier exhibitionistic twist to masturbating in front of your partner, you may want to incorporate a little hide and seek. For some people, the appeal of voyeurism is catching someone 'without their knowledge'. This is easy enough to simulate. All you need to do is get the voyeur to hide, for example in the wardrobe, and the partner to wander in, for example after a bath, then start touching themselves. Whether the voyeur is 'discovered' or not is entirely up to you. There can be a powerful sexual appeal simply in knowing that you've got someone's eyes on you but you can't see them: it's submissive and yet also controlling, as you can decide whether you're going to invite them to join you or leave them high and dry.

As a wilder alternative that works best when you live with a partner, agree that you'll both masturbate at least five times every day for a week without telling your partner when or where you'll be doing it. That way, there's a genuine risk that your lover might come home to find you on all fours with a toy sticking out of your bum, or lying on the sofa watching porn and letting your fingers roam around. And that extra frisson may be enough to spur you to even more masturbation sessions. You can agree between you what will happen when you're caught; you may want to incorporate punishment if sub/Dom appeals (of which more later), you might join in or you might simply stand in the door silently and enjoy the view.

TRUE CONFESSIONS
I KNEW HE WAS WATCHING – AND I DIDN'T CARE

On my last holiday, I had a naughty experience. I'd hired a villa with friends, and one day they wanted to go shopping and I just wanted to sunbathe, so I decided to take advantage of our suntrap balcony. I waved them off from the front door, then made myself a jug of margarita and wandered to the balcony. I poured myself a drink then stripped off, covered myself in suntan lotion and lay back to read the trashy novel I'd brought with me. The feeling of the sun on my skin was really sexy, and when I got to a passionate scene in the book, I had a naughty thought and slipped my fingers between my legs. I read the hot paragraph again and again, rubbing myself furiously until I came hard.

I felt a bit embarrassed after I came, thinking about what I'd done, but not nearly as embarrassed as I felt when I heard a grunt and turned to see a ridiculously hot guy standing on the balcony next to mine, hand on his cock having clearly just come. He blushed bright red and ran inside. I instinctively grabbed my sarong to cover myself up, but the more that I thought about him watching me as I played with myself the hornier I got. After all, I'd fancied him at first sight and it was fairly clear from his behaviour that he found me attractive too. Plucking up all my courage, I called out, 'Hello, can you come back?' and he sheepishly came out on to his balcony. I think the fact that he was a bit distant from me gave me the guts to carry on. I didn't say anything but instead started stroking my breasts, my fingers slowly circling my nipples, teasing them until they were stiff and deep pink. I looked up to see how he was reacting and he was transfixed. Even though he'd only just come I could already see the bulge rising in his shorts.

I ran the fingers of one hand over my body down to my centre, and spread my lips, before licking a finger of my other hand and slipping it inside myself. He pushed his shorts down in response, and started to tug on his thickening member. Watching him touch himself was so much hotter than just reading a sex scene in a book, and I could smell the heat of his body wafting through the air. I spread my legs wider and slipped another finger inside myself, then another as I got wetter and wetter at the thought of his eyes on me, at the sight of his stiffening cock. When he cried out once more and came, it sent me over the edge and I came hard around my fingers. He stayed there watching me for a moment or too, then returned to his room. I never got the guts up to knock on his door, but I still think about it to this day.

Jessica, 28, artist

Caught in the act

At the more extreme end of things, you may decide that you'd like to 'catch' your partner with another lover, either in reality or merely play-acting. This can be particularly effective if the woman is bicurious and her partner likes the idea of seeing her with another woman. (Or, indeed, if the man is bicurious and the woman likes the idea of seeing him with another man. According to a cliterati.co.uk poll, a third of women get off on the idea of seeing two men together so it's not as rare a fantasy as you might think.) The advantage of being caught with someone of the same sex is that it generally presents less of a threat to your partner than being caught with someone who's the same gender as they are. However, everyone's jealousy works differently so this certainly isn't a game to play unless you've talked it through together. (Follow the guidelines in Chapter Eight: Group Sex, for details on how to negotiate this.)

Regardless of the scenario, you should let the third party know the game you're playing, agree to a rough time scale for when you'll get 'caught' and agree what you'll be caught doing. Again, the voyeuristic partner might just watch (while masturbating or not), they could join in for a three-way or they could punish the 'cheating' partner for their actions. Do be careful if you play this game though – there's no point destroying a relationship for a quick sexual buzz, and you need to ensure that you know exactly what you're letting yourself in for before diving in.

TRUE CONFESSIONS
I COPPED OFF WITH A WOMAN WHILE MY LOVER WATCHED

I was seeing this guy, Will, who was a bit of a player. I really liked him, but knew that there was no way I'd get him if he saw how keen I was. Instead, I made sure that I was just as wild as he was. I talked dirty, introduced him to sub/Dom and generally played the part of a porn starlet. Don't get me wrong, it wasn't just for his benefit, as there's a nasty side of me that loves that kind of thing; but I knew that if I was going to 'win' him, I'd have to play by a new set of rules too. My dream opportunity came along in the guise of Alexandra.

I've always had a bicurious side and when I met Alex at a party and she overtly flirted with me, I certainly felt a flutter. When I asked her if she wanted to come back to my place for a cup of tea or glass of wine and she replied, 'Or we could just have sex,' I knew that she was my type of woman.

I'd already arranged for Will to come round later that night but when I told Alex, she just said: 'He can always join us.' I'd had a few threesomes before, so I wasn't averse to the idea.

Within seconds of getting home, Alex and I were kissing and within ten minutes, I was going down on her. When the doorbell went, I was almost tempted not to answer it but Alex had confessed to being bi, too, so I thought it would make things a lot more fun if Will joined us.

I kissed him hello and he pulled back, looking confused, clearly recognising the taste on my lips. 'I was just getting to know my new friend Alex,' I said. I could feel his erection press against me at my words, and pulled away. 'Glass of wine?'

I felt incredibly cool, with Alex there in a state of undress, clearly fancying me, and Will being confused but horny. He sat there drinking his wine as Alex went down on me and I alternated between groaning at her rather expert ministrations and chatting to Will as if nothing was going on. He was clearly unsure about what to do, which made me feel good as it was the first time I'd ever seen him looking out of his depth.

In the end, Alex and I took pity on him and invited him to join us. We had a fantastic night. One of my favourite memories is of him sitting at the end of the bed, wanking and smoking a cigarette, as Alex and I sixty-nined each other. From that point onwards, Will treated me with a lot more respect; I suspect that he didn't want to blow his chances of a repeat performance. However, Alex was so much more fun that I ended up dumping Will for her. Well, if it takes a man seeing you with another woman to make him pay attention, he's clearly not a real man at all, or at the very least not nearly into you enough.

Tricia, 36, insurance clerk

If You've Got It, Flaunt It: Games for Exhibitionists

There is, of course, a host of exhibitionistic games that you can play as well. Obviously, any of the voyeuristic games offers an exhibitionistic partner the opportunity to get their kicks but some games are even better suited to a lover who likes to perform.

Private dancer
While going to a strip club together can be a lot of fun, if you're more of an exhibitionist, there's nothing to stop you from dancing erotically for your partner. Indeed, you'll be tying in

with a sensual tradition, as dance has been used as an erotic aid throughout history. The ancient Romans and Greeks held sacred dances praising Bacchus and Dionysus, in which naked women danced around a pole decorated with ivy, vine leaves and honeycomb – an early precursor to pole dancing. Unlike your average pole-dancing club, however, these dances were often followed by an orgy.

Nowadays, things are a bit more civilised (or less fun, depending on how you look at it). While there is no shortage of opportunities should you choose to get naked and grind in front of a crowd (either with or without a pole), over the last decade or so, a wealth of companies has sprung up offering striptease, burlesque and pole-dancing lessons, DVDs and home pole-dancing kits. All you need to do is spend a little time and money and you'll be able to grind and gyrate with the best of them, offering your partner a wanton view of your body.

According to Queendom.com, over a third of women have put on strip shows for their partner and about the same number again would like to give it a go. And it's not just something for the female of the species. The same research found that a third of men strip for their partners at least occasionally, and over 40 per cent would like to. That's a lot of wannabe Chippendales waiting in the wings.

If you don't want to go on a course, performing a basic striptease is a relatively easy skill to teach yourself. The most important thing to remember is that the tease is as important as the strip – if not more so.

Start by preparing the scene. There's no point doing a striptease in a cluttered room; falling over a pizza box as you strip will hardly make you feel sexy, so make sure the room is tidy. Make the lighting low, either with fairy lights or lamps, but avoid candles, as they can present a fire risk when you're flinging your undies away with abandon. Pick the music that you're going to perform to and practise your routine when your lover is out of the house so that it's as slick as it can possibly be. You should also apply thought to what you're wearing and avoid clothes that are difficult to remove. For women this includes corsets (unless they zip up), shoes with complicated fastenings and anything that's so tight that you need to wriggle out of it. For men, leave your socks off (there's no way to make them look sexy), avoid lace-up shoes (unless they can be left undone with the laces tucked safely inside them) and don't wear a shirt with cufflinks unless you can slip it off easily without having to remove them.

Although your routine depends entirely on which bits of your body you want to show off, and how comfortable you feel dancing for your partner, the following guidelines will make you look a lot slicker:

- **Maintain eye contact with your partner.** Don't stare at them, but let them see how much you fancy them when you look into their eyes. Alternate this with looking at whichever item of clothing you're removing to draw attention to the part of your body you want your partner to look at.

- **Don't rush.** Although you may feel nervous, don't hurry through trying to get your kit off as quickly as possible. Instead, give your lover a brief flash before covering yourself once more: hide your bits with items of clothes you've removed, turn your back the second you've flashed your breasts or genitals, then give a cheeky wink over your shoulder. Or you could use a prop, like a feather boa, to cover your assets. The longer you make your lover wait for the eventual 'reveal', the hotter they'll feel when you finally show them everything. Whether you opt for a 'no touching' policy is entirely up to you.

The pole's the goal

If you want to twirl upside down, do the splits in mid-air and generally be a pole-dancing diva, it definitely makes sense to take a few lessons with a reputable teacher so that you know how to do so safely. A full pole-dancing session is a lot more demanding than striptease and you don't want to damage your-self – injuries can include head trauma from bashing yourself on the pole, spinal bruising from writhing against it, scabs on the knees from sliding across the floor, bruises from gripping the pole, bunions and corns from wearing uncomfortable heels, shin splints from supporting your body weight, back pain, damaged discs from tossing your hair around and even ruptured breast implants from crashing into the pole too hard. As such, you don't want to attempt an ambitious routine unless you know what you're letting yourself in for.

That said, these injuries generally affect people who pole dance for a living rather than casual users. Generally, recreational pole dancing is a fun way to tone up and get a bit kinky. Indeed, much has been made of the health benefits of pole dancing, which include burning calories, toning up your arms, abs, shoulders and legs and improving flexibility – not to mention boosting confidence.

Don't even think about pole dancing, however, when you've had anything to drink (which, let's face it, will be the most tempting time), and make sure you spend time practising alone before you perform for your partner. You won't exactly look your sexiest if your moves are ungainly (though you may look endearingly cute).

Oh, and don't think that pole dancing is just for women. There are now companies offering pole-dancing lessons for men too, so if the idea of watching your man writhing around a giant pole does it for you, he's got no excuse not to give it a go.

Out and about

Of course, exhibitionism doesn't have to involve striptease. Having sex outdoors is an incredibly common kinky fantasy that has elements of exhibitionism about it. Even if the idea of *actually* being caught fills you with dread, the risk that some-one might see what you're doing is an inherent part of the appeal.

When it comes to making your fantasy come true, however, you need to be careful. As mentioned earlier, public nudity is illegal in many parts of the world, and if you're caught in the act you could get yourself arrested for indecent exposure or worse. Plus, sexy as it can be to get down to it outdoors, you need to be mindful of other people: you don't want a family walking past just as you reach the point of no return.

Given the risks of outdoor sex, it makes sense to either pick a location that's very isolated or be incredibly discreet so that nobody knows what you're doing. If you opt for the former, you could go for the middle of the countryside (but check first that you haven't inadvertently picked a 'dogging' location – unless, of course, you like the idea of getting it on while other people watch and join in). Beaches can be great outdoor sex locations if you go very late at night or early in the morning (no later than 4 or 5 a.m. or you run the risk of being caught by fishermen) and make sure that you take two blankets: one to protect you from the sand and the other to protect your modesty. If you've got mega-bucks, you could always go on holiday to a private island and take advantage of your solitude. Then again, if you're that rich, you could probably afford a good enough lawyer that you could have sex in the middle of the street and still get away with it.

If you live in a city and can't get out to the middle of nowhere, go for the discretion approach instead. This is mostly down to being prepared. Make sure that you wear clothes that allow easy access to your bits: for the woman, a long jacket, short skirt and hold-ups with no knickers; for the man, a long coat and button-fly jeans (you don't want to risk a zip-getting-caught incident should you need to make a quick getaway).

Choose a location that allows you to appear as if you're simply admiring the view, such as a bridge overlooking a river or the roof garden of a cocktail bar that overlooks the city. The woman should then 'warm herself up' with some discreet toy play, either nipping off to nearby toilets or, alternatively, using a quiet vibrator over her clothes, letting her jacket hide what she's doing. (Keep a quiet miniature bullet vibrator in your handbag for instant foreplay on the go; you'll probably find it gets you ready for action infinitely quicker than your fingers.)

Once the woman is suitably aroused, she should stand in front of the man and let him nuzzle into her, pressing his (still jean-clad) bits against her buttocks to help him ready for action (alternatively, he can go to the loo to warm himself at the same time as she does). Once he's 'up for it', he should slip the condom on, using his coat to hide what he's doing, then enter the woman from behind, wrapping his coat around her so that it simply looks as if they are enjoying an affectionate cuddle. Quick and dirty is the aim of the game here, so use every trick that you can muster to take things to the logical conclusion as fast as possible. The woman can clench her kegel muscles, use the bullet vibrator on her clitoris or his perineum and cross her legs to tighten her vagina; the man can whisper erotic inspiration in the woman's ear, use his finger on her clit (hidden by her jacket) or play with her breasts under her jacket. For an extra bit of extra kink, the woman could wear nipple clamps with a chain between them to connect them underneath her top. That way the man can easily stimulate both nipples simply by tugging on the chain.

Taking a packet of intimate wipes with you so that you can clean up quickly and easily once you're done will make your walk home a lot more pleasant (particularly if you don't use condoms with your partner). Then again, there can be a submissive thrill in enjoying the 'walk of shame' once you've got away with the al fresco action, feeling your lover's juices trickling down your thigh. So if power play and humiliation float your boat, leave the baby wipes at home.

'Before going to stand in line at the movies, cut holes in your pockets. Then you can diddle in the queue.'

Annie Sprinkle, ex-prostitute and porn star and PhD sexologist

It's only natural

If having sex outdoors is a little too daring for you, but you still like the idea of showing yourself off, another option is to explore naturism. While many naturists indulge purely because they enjoy the feeling of sun on their skin and the wind ruffling their body hair, rather than for any sexual kick, there are also people who are on the scene because they have voyeuristic or exhibitionistic desires.

As long as you respect people around you and don't ogle anyone unless it's clear that they're happy to be observed, there are numerous naturist beaches you can go to all over the world. Alternatively, you could book yourself a holiday at a naturist resort and spend a whole week or longer naked. Be careful when choosing your naturist resort though: some have no sexual aspect whatsoever and simply allow people the freedom to wander around naked (which may be perfect for you if you're new to the whole 'getting naked in public' thing and don't want to get propositioned by strangers); others, however, are overtly sexual. You can generally tell what kind of naturist resort you're going to by checking their website or brochure first; if it mentions adult party games or kinky club nights, it's going to be at the salacious end of the spectrum; if it lists naked swimming, darts and ballroom dancing, less so. There are pros and cons for both, and you need to pick the one that you think will best suit you and your partner.

EMILY'S EXPERIENCES: *NATURIST HEAVEN, NATURIST HELL*

I've had two naturist experiences – one great, one horrible. The first was at a naked disco called, aptly enough, Starkers. I went along unsure about what to expect, with my then boyfriend and my best friend in tow.

Stripping off in the changing rooms at the club was easier than I thought it would be. I was more concerned about my friend seeing my man naked than I was about anyone seeing me. However, once we got into the main venue, I felt a little more uncomfortable, not least because the seats were leather which is hardly ideal against naked skin.

My friend and I started chatting to each other to try to ignore the absurdity of the situation. After a minute or so we forgot that we were naked – until we looked up to see men to our left, to our right, straight ahead of us, all gradually getting closer to the sofa we were sitting on. Suddenly, we realised we were the only women in the venue. We headed upstairs, walking sideways so as not to give any of the men a particularly graphic view, got ourselves some drinks and carried on blathering. Half an hour later, we'd met some really nice people and were surprised to find that it wasn't lecherous at all. By the end of the night we felt uncomfortable putting our clothes back on – it's amazing how restrictive they seem when you've spent an evening naked – and I was a convert to the naturism scene. Or so I thought.

Later that year, I was invited to cover a naturist holiday for a feature. I arrived at the destination (I won't say where because I'm sure the experience was down to my particular tour rep rather than the resort in general) and within twenty minutes of arriving had been asked by said tour rep, 'Are you a sexpert or a dirty slut?' Given that he was wearing an 'FBI: Female Body Inspector' T-shirt at the time, it didn't really put me at ease. As we waited at the airport for the rest of the party to arrive, my heart sank more and more. Each new addition seemed older, more obese and more lecherous, the pièce de résistance being the guy who was so infirm that he defecated in his pants on the way to the villa.

The week only got worse from that point on. When I

interviewed the naturists (all male), one said he enjoyed the holidays because he got to look at naked women, while another kept trying to persuade me to let him photograph me. When I got my period on the third day, meaning that I had an excuse to wear a sarong, I was incredibly relieved. By the end of the week, I'd spent more than one night in tears and had almost flown home three times.

I wouldn't say that it put me off naturism, as there's still something pleasant about stripping off and feeling the sun on your skin (as long as you've got factor 50 on your sensitive bits), but I'd be very careful in future when it came to choosing the tour group and the resort. I'm sure that the guys on the trip had a whale of a time but for a woman in her early thirties, without an older-man obsession, it was truly the week from hell.

Performing for an audience

One of the kinkiest levels of exhibitionism is having sex in front of other people and *not* trying to get away with it, instead revelling in their gaze. Obviously, this isn't the kind of thing that's likely to happen down the local pub (unless it has a very open-minded landlord), but there are numerous events you can attend that cater to this desire.

Start by searching the Internet for fetish clubs in your area. While some discourage nudity and only allow kinky play rather than full-on sex, others take a broader view and have more of an 'anything goes' policy. Check the rules and regulations for the fetish night and it should be clear enough which category each club fits into.

'Go to clubs but be aware of the etiquette. Make sure you're not offending anyone by watching'.

Mistress Absolute, professional Dominatrix

Swinging nights are another option. Contrary to many people's belief, there's no obligation to have sex with other people at a swinging party; many couples go along simply to have sex in front of other people, watch other people have sex and generally enjoy the whole liberated environment. You'll probably be approached by other people who want to 'play' with you, but all good swinging clubs have strict 'No means no' guidelines, so all you need to do is decline, then carry on having sex with other people watching, safe in the knowledge that the only hands you'll feel on your body will be your lover's. (*See* Chapter Eight: Group Sex, for more about swinging events.)

TIPS FROM THE SCENE

There is exhibitionism and there is exhibitionism with touching, where the audience gets to grope. Decide in advance what you think about this, and enact a scenario where you are likely to get what you want without being disappointed in the voyeurs' behaviour.

Mark, founder of swinging website and event, FeverParties.com

If one or both of you feels perturbed at the idea of having sex in the same room as other people, but still get a thrill at the idea of being watched, use technology to your advantage. You could make a porn film together and edit it so that you're not identifiable (some things are best kept private – you wouldn't want a future boss seeing clips of you cavorting with your lover, unless, that is, you want to be a porn star). Then, upload it on to one of the numerous other 'user generated content' adult websites.

Alternatively, if you want to be watched 'live', simply hook up a webcam and broadcast what you're doing over the Internet. You can almost guarantee that you'll find a more than willing audience, but you could always advertise what you're doing through a kinky Internet forum if you want to be sure of having people to watch you.

As with cybersex, it's worth protecting your identity, either by keeping your face out of shot, along with any other distinctive markings (such as tattoos or unusual piercings) or by wearing wigs or masks to change the way you look (think masked ball rather than Goofy or George Bush; some things will just instantly kill the mood). Make sure that the microphone is switched off so that you don't give yourself away through you voice either. Then let yourself go and enjoy being watched, safe in the knowledge that your exploits will be a sexy secret that only you and your partner will share.

TRUE CONFESSIONS

A LESBIAN FRIEND WATCHED US SHAGGING

I've always liked the idea of being watched and directed by a third party during sex, but I hate the idea of anyone but me touching my man, so I'd resigned myself to the fact that it was never going to happen. My boyfriend Scott knew that it was a turn-on for me though, so he'd often whisper that he could see someone looking at us through the curtains, gesturing at me to move my hips faster, wrap my legs around him or start sucking him. It wasn't as hot as I imagined the real thing would be, but it was close enough to keep me happy.

Then one night, we were out with my lesbian friend, Emma. She'd been single for about two years and was complaining about how horny she was. We were all quite tipsy, and I joked that I'd lend her Scott but I didn't think he was her type. Emma blushed and confessed that she was so desperate she'd started having fantasies she'd never had before: not about having sex with a man, but about watching a couple get it on. 'I've tried watching porn,' she said, 'but that isn't enough. I want to know what it's really like, what it smells like, what a real orgasm looks like and porn hardly does that.'

Scott looked at me and raised his eyebrow. I knew exactly what he was thinking and felt my juices start to bubble up at the idea. Emma wasn't my type and I knew that Scott didn't fancy her either, so I didn't feel threatened by the idea of her being in the room while he and I got it on.

'You could always watch us,' I said.

'Let's do it,' was her instant response. We hurried home, and Scott and I stripped off the second we were indoors: we didn't want to lose the momentum.

Scott went down on me in the front room as Emma sat on the sofa and watched us. There was a brief embarrassing moment when the time came to have sex and he fumbled with the condom – I didn't know what to say and pretended Emma wasn't there – but when he was inside me and I could hear Emma moaning, I felt really horny. She didn't tell us what to do so it wasn't quite our perfect fantasy, but when Scott and I heard her coming, it set us both off.

Afterwards it was a bit embarrassing and she went home, but the next time we saw her it was fine. We didn't mention it but I still think about it every now and again.

Christine, 35, traffic warden

Are You Ready For More?

Now that you've started to explore the delights you can enjoy through watching and being watched, whether by strangers or simply by your lover, you may decide to leave it there (or, indeed, decide that it's not for you). But if you like the idea of delving deeper still into the fetish world, you might want to start adding some props into the equation. Don't worry, we're not getting into whips and chains and pointy things quite yet; we'll start with a prop that everyone has easily available, with no visits to a sex shop required.

Yes, we're moving into food play. And while aphrodisiac

meals and *9½ Weeks* fantasies may seem a little tame to be included in a fetish book, trust me: by the time you've explored the world of the sushi girl or entered the paddling pool of custard that is sploshing, you'll see exactly how kinky food can be. So, make sure your larder is fully stocked, grab my hand once again and be prepared to get your appetite utterly sated. I promise I won't bite.

CHAPTER THREE

Food Play

Great sex is about getting in touch with all your senses, so it's hardly surprising that food play is a common kink, whether that's drizzling maple syrup over the breasts of your beloved, turning your partner into a creamy dessert then licking every bit of them clean, feeding them treats *9½ Weeks*-style or wrestling them in custard. Some people even get off on the idea of simulated cannibalism (or vore, *see* p. 119).

Obviously, this is one of the more extreme forms of food play, while for most people the fetish is a lot less contrived. However, messing around with food is something that's increasingly entering the mainstream. The *Sex and the City* film saw Samantha lying back, naked and covered in raw fish as a sexy sushi platter for her man, and there are high-class party planners who offer (generally rich) people the opportunity to book naked men and women covered in everything from cream teas to curry for their parties (seriously – just hope for the 'platter's sake that it's not a vindaloo, although ginger can be used for kinky food play, of which more later).

At the more affordable end of the spectrum, you can buy edible sex products of every type from sensual chocolate sauces specifically designed for sex to erotic cream-whipping devices, and from oral sex sprays to flavoured lubricants. And that's before you even get into the vast world of aphrodisiacs; something that was written about in the very earliest of sex manuals.

When it comes down to it, sex and food both satisfy basic human hungers, so it only makes sense to at least give the world of food play a little nibble. You can always burn the extra calories off in the sack afterwards.

'Food play is messy fun. People are really freaked out by it sometimes because we are taught not to play with food, but that's what's so great about it. We are going against our upbringing and it's all safe sex!'

**Annie Sprinkle, ex-prostitute and porn star
and PhD sexologist**

Feeling Hungry?

One of the joys of food play, from a kinky point of view, is that the entry level is really quite 'vanilla': you don't need to face up to scary insights from your psyche, risk any pain or even share anything particularly saucy with your partner (except, perhaps, for a drizzle of strawberry coulis).

You can start with something as simple as using lotions and

potions to sweeten oral sex, or preparing each other an aphrodisiac feast as an easy way to recognise the seductive power of food. However, if you find that feeding all your senses gets you off, there are numerous ways that you can develop the kink: by being a platter for your lover; by playing sub/Dom games in which your blindfolded partner has to guess what they're eating or face the consequences; by having a food fight; or going the whole hog and entering the messy world of sploshing, in which you cover your partner in custard, cream pies and even baked beans (and probably get covered yourself). But before we get to that, let's start with something much tamer: using lotions and potions to enhance your sexual experience.

Adding flavour to your passion

Tasting your lover's most intimate juices can be a wonderful way for you to bond with each other. And while the body's natural scent is a key way to attract a partner (at a subliminal level, we're drawn to people whose pheromones – the chemicals used to attract a mate – suggest they have a complementary immune system to our own), changing the way that you smell and taste can add a little spice to your relationship. That's not to say that you need to mask your natural taste – there's absolutely nothing wrong with the taste of healthy juices – but simply, that you can use a multitude of substances to ring the changes.

If your juices don't taste pleasant, or you don't like the way that your partner tastes, there can be a number of causes. Alcohol and cigarettes both tend to make sexual juices taste bitter, while curry and asparagus will both pass their distinctive tastes on. Dehydration can lead to thicker juices which some people find distasteful, and a generally unhealthy diet will also show itself in the way that you taste.

Pineapple juice is well known as a good way to sweeten

semen (just drink a pint every morning and you'll probably be rewarded with much more oral sex), and most fruits also help make things taste more pleasant. So getting your 'five a day' is good for your sex life as well as your health. You can also buy substances that are designed to sweeten the taste of natural juices. However, the instructions for most of these products recommend that you drink them with lots of water or masturbate before and after using them, both of which are liable to sweeten the juices anyway, so take any claims you read with a pinch of salt; a bowl of fruit salad is just as likely to do the job and at a fraction of the cost.

Obviously, ensuring that you've washed properly down below is only polite if you're expecting any kind of oral action too. After all, you wouldn't eat dinner off a dirty plate so why expect your lover to dine in when the washing-up hasn't been done?

Assuming that you aren't trying to mask the taste, but are simply trying to mix things up a bit, there are numerous substances that you can use for food play. At one end of the spectrum are regular foodstuffs like cream, chocolate sauce and ice cream (of which more later). While these can be used during oral sex, you do need to ensure that you wash scrupulously afterwards, as lingering sugars can lead to yeast infections. You also need to be wary about getting too experimental. One of the most unpleasant sexual injuries I ever heard about relates to a couple who, for some insane (probably alcohol-motivated) reason, decided to use tuna in food play. The man inserted it into the woman, then proceeded to eat it out of her. So far, so nasty. But the real 'eugh' moment came a few weeks later when the woman suffered crippling pelvic pains. On examination by the doctor, it turned out that the man had been less than scrupulous about removing the tuna and it had rotted inside her, taking half her cervix with it. Every time I share that story

I find myself crossing my legs, but it acts as a good warning to be very careful about what you use in sex play; the result, otherwise, can be very damaging.

As a much safer alternative, opt for whipped cream (though again, avoid using it internally as that's just asking for trouble, and as it contains fat there's also a risk that it could break a condom). You can buy erotic cream-whipping devices if cream becomes a regular feature in your sex life. Best of all, invest in a product that's been tested for use down below, such as a flavoured lubricant. You can get sampler packs containing different types of lube so that you can find a flavour that suits you both. Some will additionally make your bits tingle (mint being particularly common) or warm up (cinnamon often being the flavour) which can add a new edge to proceedings.

Oral sex sprays are another option. These come in flavours including cherry, tingly mint and the somewhat scary sounding (but actually quite hot) chocolate-chilli, and are specifically designed for use on the genitals, so are also less likely to cause irritation.

EMILY'S EXPERIENCES: I TEST SEX FLAVOURINGS FOR A LIVING

When I'm not off experiencing the fetish scene for work, I spend my time writing features about sex, and have reviewed countless sex products over the last few years. Whenever a flavoured lube or sex spray turns up, I am slightly sceptical as I've tasted so many hideous ones that, frankly, I've found most products more likely to detract from oral sex than enhance it.

Chocolate spreads are by far the worse culprits (or maybe it's because I'm a chocolate snob). Most tend to be made from the cheapest chocolate available – that's if they contain any cocoa solids at all – and are sickly sweet, making you feel nauseous long before you feel frisky. There's also a product called sex chocolate that's designed to enhance libido, but when we tried it in the *Scarlet* office, all five of the women sampling it got headachy or aggressive, so I wouldn't race to try it again. I'd recommend that, rather than buying an overpriced bottle of chocolate body sauce, you simply get some good-quality chocolate and melt it yourself, making sure that it's cooled down enough not to cause burns when you use it, of course (never melt chocolate intended for sex play in the microwave as it can carry on heating up after it's removed).

Flavoured lubes can be fantastic, depending on which you get. When I've run seduction seminars, I've often passed around bottles of different types of lube and asked women to taste them all to see which they like best. There are never consistent answers, just going to show that everyone has different tastes, so it's only really by trying lots of different types that you can get an idea of what's best for you (don't forget to get your partner to taste it too; they can be used on men and women). It can also make for a sexy evening, if you put dabs of the various flavours on yourself then ask your partner to lick them off as part of the 'taste test'.

And the sex sprays can be dreadful or incredible. I've found that, as a general rule, if something claims to contain pheromones or increase libido, it'll be at the headachy end of the spectrum, whereas if it's nothing more than a flavoured spray, it's more likely to be pleasant. Of course, there's nothing to stop you from making your own spray with, say, cherry juice in a standard spray bottle. However, the sex sprays are less likely to include sugars, which can cause irritation, so if you do go for the DIY option then make sure you shower thoroughly afterwards.

An aphrodisiac feast

Of course, food doesn't have to be applied to the body in order to be sexy. One of the oldest sex tips recommended in the very earliest sex manuals, including the *Kama Sutra*, is to create an aphrodisiac feast to enjoy with your partner. After all, what better way to pamper the one you love than by preparing a romantic meal? (You can always enjoy your partner for dessert.)

While the jury is out on whether or not aphrodisiacs actually work, there is at least some logic behind the idea of many of them. With certain aphrodisiacs, their reputation stems from their shape: for example, oysters and figs (cut in half) are thought to resemble a woman's genitals, while bananas and asparagus are obviously phallic. However, there are other, more scientific reasons as to why these could have benefits. Oysters are high in zinc which is essential for semen production, while figs are high in vitamin B which is essential for the synthesis of sex hormones. (They are also rumoured to be the 'forbidden fruit' from the Garden of Eden and are thrown instead of confetti in some European countries to bestow fertility – and, no doubt, irritate the bride whose dress is getting spattered in fruit.) Bananas are high in potassium, which is important for healthy sex hormone production, and asparagus is high in vitamin C which also helps to make healthy sex hormones and neurotransmitters.

And those are just a few of the reputed aphrodisiacs available. Chocolate helps your body release endorphins, and is also one of the few food products that melt at body temperature, creating an extra sensuality around eating it. Carrots are high in vitamin A as well as being phallic. Chilli and ginger are both thought to increase blood flow to the genitals and 'heat the loins', although whether you'd want to get it on with someone who's been gorging on chilli is another matter entirely. Any form of seafood is good for the libido, for the same reason as oysters (and not, as some crude types might joke, down to any relation between fish and female genitalia). And, if you team the seafood with champagne, you will, reputedly, get a double whammy of aphrodisiac power because the scent of sparkling wine, particularly blanc de blancs, is rumoured to replicate women's natural pheromones. For dessert, opt for pineapple. It's not only high in vitamin C but, as mentioned before, will impart its semen-sweetening properties. (The man has to eat the pineapple, obviously; it doesn't have the power to change the way that female taste buds work, but it does blast away funky spunk.)

Choose from the menus below, all of which contain a wide selection of aphrodisiacs. If you're no good at cooking, you can buy most of them ready made in the shops, although obviously, the fresher the ingredients and the less additives the dish contains, the stronger the effects are likely to be. So opt for the most natural version that you can muster.

MENU 1

· · · · ·

Celery soup with white truffle oil

If you make your own celery soup, make sure that you strain it before serving, otherwise it can be too stringy and bits of celery between the teeth aren't a good look. If you buy ready-made celery soup, go for a carton rather than a can, and garnish with a splash of white truffle oil, which is easily available from most delicatessens. (It may seem pricey, but a small bottle will last you a long time, so it's worth the expense. One whiff of the musky aroma and you'll understand why it's thought to be an aphrodisiac.)

Fresh lobster served with rocket salad

There's no need to cook the lobster from scratch unless you're a keen chef. If you are going to cook it yourself, however, check your partner's ethical viewpoint on lobster as some people (women in particular) are squeamish about cooking lobsters from live, as they feel it's cruel. (The 'scream' the lobster makes is actually air escaping rather than a cry of pain but it can be less than libido-enhancing to hear screams coming from the kitchen, while you await your romantic meal.) You can kill the lobster before cooking it by putting a pin through the cross in its forehead. Alternatively, buy a pre-prepared lobster from a supermarket or fishmonger. Serve with garlic mayonnaise. Garlic is thought to be an aphrodisiac as it thins the blood and boosts circulation, so as long as you don't mind the smell (in which case it can be a passion killer), it's a good addition. Alternatively, put a layer of chilli or ginger butter over the lobster and grill it. Serve with rocket salad as it's a good source of vitamin C.

Dark chocolate mousse

One of the best-known aphrodisiacs, a chocolate dessert is bound to go down well. It's easy enough to make a cheat's version of chocolate mousse by whipping some double cream, folding in melted chocolate and adding a slug of brandy or cream liqueur to pack an extra punch. Alternatively, buy a good-quality chocolate mousse that's made using chocolate with high cocoa solids. Serve with stem ginger (unless you used it with the lobster, in which case it'll be ginger overkill) to give the dish more aphrodisiac power.

MENU 2

· · · · ·

Caviar and sour cream blinis

If caviar is out of your budget, lumpfish roe is a good alternative. Although you can make the blinis yourself, you can get perfectly good ready-made ones that need only to be heated under the grill. Top with the sour cream and a spoonful of the roe or caviar, sprinkle with chives and serve with a lemon wedge for the full effect. Caviar is ideal teamed with champagne or sparkling wine. Alternatively, serve with a shot of frozen honey vodka (freezing it thickens the vodka and makes it taste smoother). The honey will add another aphrodisiac layer to the dish. Just don't go overboard with it; getting inebriated so early in your meal will scupper your romantic chances.

Scallops with chilli and ginger

Scallops do require a little effort, as it's very hard to find ready-made scallop dishes that are worth eating. However, for an average-sized scallop all you need to do is:

- Heat a teaspoon of sunflower oil in a pan with a finely chopped chilli and a teaspoon of finely chopped fresh ginger, until it's smoking but not burned.

- Part dry your scallops on kitchen paper (make sure they are all the same size, otherwise some will be rubbery and others undercooked) then put them in the pan for about 60 seconds per side. If they're small scallops (ask your fishmonger if you're unsure about size) cook them for less time, and if they're large cook them for a little longer. It's better to undercook rather than overcook them, as you can eat them rare but they turn to rubber if they're overcooked. Season with a sprinkle of salt and take them out.

- Put some butter in the pan and warm through, add a squeeze of lemon juice, then pour over the scallops.

Pineapple carpaccio

This is an impressive name for finely sliced pineapple. Simply take a fresh pinapple, remove the skin and core then slice into pieces about 2mm thick. Sprinkle with brown sugar and put under a very hot grill until the sugar bubbles or, alternatively, pour over a couple of spoonfuls of rum and leave to marinate for around two hours. Chinese five spice is also a good libido-enhancing addition to the dish. Serve with premium vanilla pod ice cream for another aphrodisiac layer.

MENU 3

· · · · ·

Asparagus with melted butter

Heat an oiled griddle pan with sunflower oil and lay your asparagus on it. Cook for about five minutes per side (or less, if you're using fine asparagus), then transfer to a plate and pour over melted butter. Fresh coriander, lemon juice or Parmesan (but not all three) are all nice additions, although if you opt for Parmesan use olive oil rather than melted butter to drizzle over the asparagus. Eat with your fingers or, better still, serve your partner for some finger-sucking fun.

Garlic mushroom filo parcels

You can buy ready-made mushroom parcels, then drizzle with truffle oil for extra sensuality. Or make your own using ready-made filo pastry which you fill with a mixture of mushrooms fried in olive oil with onions or leeks and finished with garlic butter. Brush the parcels with melted butter and cook according to the instructions on the pastry packet. Serve with a rocket salad.

Honey and lavender crème brûlée

Buy ready made crème brûlée and dress the plate with lavender honey. Alternatively, make it from scratch, following a recipe of your choice, but using lavender honey in place of the sugar in the custard. Garnish with an organic lavender flower (non-organic ones may have been sprayed with harmful pesticides).

MENU 4

. . . . .

Fresh oysters

Simply shuck them (ask your fishmonger to show you how), then serve on a plate of crushed ice with a sauce of sherry vinegar and finely chopped shallots.

Clam and saffron linguini

You can buy ready-made clam sauce, but it's far nicer to buy your own clams, steam them (having first soaked them in water to remove the grit), then fold through fresh spaghetti that you've boiled with saffron (so that the colour tints the pasta). Sprinkle with lots of freshly chopped parsley or chives and finish with a mild olive oil.

Stem ginger ice cream

Buy a ready-made premium ice cream and serve with the syrup from a jar of stem ginger and some brandy snaps. Fresh fruit will add to the aphrodisiac appeal, with bananas being a particularly good match. You can also drizzle with chocolate sauce or grate over fresh chocolate for a truly decadent dessert.

There's no guarantee that any of these menus will work as an aphrodisiac, but if you set the scene with candlelight and soft music, get dressed up in your sexiest outfit, with even sexier underwear, flirt with your lover over dinner and make sure you don't drink too much alcohol (Shakespeare was right when he said it increases desire but lessens performance), there's a good chance that you'll end up having fabulous sex later the same night. And that's what making an aphrodisiac meal is all about.

Dinner's on me

The ancient Japanese tradition of *nyotaimori* (otherwise known as being a sushi platter) shot to fame courtesy of the *Sex and the City* film, as mentioned earlier, but it's actually been around for hundreds of years. Although *nyotaimori* is traditionally a female role, whereby women are trained to withstand prolonged exposure to cold food and lie down for hours without moving, it can be equally enjoyable nibbling exquisite treats from a man's body.

And there's no reason why you have to stick to sushi. If you're not a fan of raw fish, you could 'dress' your partner as an erotic dessert smothered with cream (or, if you're feeling cruel, ice cream), fresh fruit and chocolate sauce. You could opt for creating a cream tea on your partner, with miniature sandwiches, scones, jam and clotted cream. Or you could go for a healthy fresh fruit salad and cover your lover in cherries, strawberries, slices of fresh nectarine and grapes (cut in half to stop them rolling off). Avoid citrus fruits though, as they can sting. And, whichever option you go for, put a latex sheet down first; you don't want your bed sheets to smell if you get so turned on that you just have to get it on before you've finished your meal.

If you like the idea of indulging in *nyotaimori*, prepare all the food in advance, ideally the night before, unless it's something that will suffer from being in the fridge overnight; you don't want to risk being so flustered by cooking that you lose your libido. Unless you're feeling particularly unkind (or you're using food that goes off really quickly) take everything out of the fridge an hour before you eat so that it can warm up to room temperature and feel less uncomfortable on your lover's skin. Then bathe your partner so that they're scrupulously clean. This can also, obviously, act as foreplay, making your meal much more highly charged with erotic anticipation. If you feel like really pampering your partner, you can also give them a sensual massage, using sunflower oil, as that won't pass on any flavour, before laying the food on their body as elegantly as you can. Your partner should avoid wearing any perfume or aftershave, as these will taint the meal.

Once you've 'prepared' your partner, take a picture (assuming your lover consents) to immortalise your work, then dive in and start eating. Don't forget to feed your partner too; not only will this make them feel appreciated, it will also stop you from feeling too bloated to get frisky once you're done. Alternatively, you could go for the somewhat messier option of having sex with your partner once they're covered in food. All that slipping and sliding could well add an extra frisson.

EMILY'S EXPERIENCES: I WAS A NAKED PARTY PLATTER

One of my more intriguing assignments was spending a night as a sushi platter. I had to go to a private members' club and, having showered thoroughly, strip down to my underwear (traditional sushi girls are naked but I have my limits) and lie down to be 'dressed' by the 'sushi mistress'.

She arranged the fish in an exquisite pattern on my body but had problems when it came to dressing my breasts: the rice blocks kept falling off, so I ended up with sashimi draped over my breasts instead as it stayed on more easily. She then put a glass of chopsticks in one hand, a glass of soy sauce in the other and poured a pool of soy sauce into my navel. I balked at the wasabi, so she left that on the side for people to add if they wanted it.

The trickiest part was staying still (even the shallowest breathing made the sushi fall off), and hearing people chatting around me as they arrived at the party, but not being able to respond, was incredibly objectifying (although I have to admit that it was interesting – and slightly hot).

Once her work of art was complete, the sushi mistress announced that dinner was served and the guests dived in, starting off using chopsticks, but soon nibbling the sushi and sashimi directly off my bare skin. They were respectful (no one tried to get in any sneaky gropes, but one man did pinch my nipple with his chopsticks – accidentally, or so he claimed) and the whole experience was interesting, if a little chilly.

When every last piece of sushi had been eaten off my body, I nipped to the toilets for a wash (the smell of sushi on skin is not good after you've been covered in it for an hour) and headed home. I could see the appeal; there was a certain exhibitionistic thrill in being naked and yet not treated as a sexual object. But stopping myself from laughing at the surreal situation was a nightmare.

I'd definitely recommend trying *nyotaimori* with a partner, but I'd suggest that you go for fruit rather than fish, unless you're prepared to lower your body temperature to such an extent that you'd be shivering – warm sushi just doesn't taste right (a couple of guests fed me some of the sushi from my own body) and the smell is far from sexy.

Feed me

Here's an option that's halfway between simply having a meal and being objectified as a sexual platter. Ever since *9½ Weeks* first hit the cinema screens, couples have been emulating the classic scene in which Mickey Rourke blindfolds Kim Basinger and feeds her a selection of nice – and not so nice – nibbles. It combines submission and domination, with food fetish giving it a potentially kinkier twist than standard food play alone.

It's easy enough to replicate the scene. Simply tie and/or bind your partner, then feed them a selection of different foods that you've set up on a tray beforehand. The key here is to make sure that your partner is unaware of what they're being fed (having first checked to ensure that they don't have any allergies: a peanut-induced anaphylactic shock rarely acts as a good aphrodisiac). Alternate sweet treats like fresh strawberries with savoury nibbles like olives and, if you feel cruel, throw in some surprises like a jalapeno pepper or a piece of fresh ginger (both are considered to be aphrodisiacs, but that doesn't make them any more pleasant on the palate).

If you're a gourmet, consider making a selection of canapés to feed your partner rather than simply opting for 'ready-to-go' treats. If your partner is a foodie too, you can add frisson to the game by asking them to name all the ingredients you've used to make the canapés: if they get it right, they win a sexual reward but if they get it wrong, they have to pay a sexual forfeit. You can add extra spices to each dish, or deliberately use obscure ingredients, so that it's harder for your partner to get it right. Some options for sensual canapés with an aphrodisiac twist include:

- a shot glass of celeriac soup with freshly grated white truffle

- asparagus wrapped in Parma ham

- smoked salmon and sour cream blinis

- oven-roasted tomatoes with garlic, mozzarella and basil oil

- baked new potatoes with sour cream and caviar

- lobster ravioli with lemon butter sauce

- chocolate-dipped strawberries

- banana dipped in caramel sauce

- watermelon chunks soaked in vodka

- honeydew melon soaked in port

- mango ice cream served in half a lychee.

Alternatively, if you like the idea of teasing your partner with decadent treats but lack any form of cooking skills, most of the above (or similar) can be bought ready-made from gourmet food stores. Just garnish them carefully at home and they'll taste almost as good as something you've made yourself.

TRUE CONFESSIONS

MY CHEF BOYFRIEND SATISFIED MY APPETITE FOR KINKY PLAY

I've always been a bit of a foodie but I'd never seen it as a particularly sexual thing. Sure, it can be nice cooking someone a meal or vice versa, but that's more about romance than sex for me. Then I met Callum. He was training to be a chef at the time (he's subsequently gone on to own his own restaurant) and told me that he wanted to cook me a special meal. He knew how important food is to me – we'd had an hour long conversation about the rise of pea shoots as a garnish the night we met – so I thought he was just going to show off his talents. He did.

When I arrived, Callum told me that he didn't want me to have any food prejudices so he was going to blind-fold me. I was a little surprised but agreed. I trusted him, and there's nothing that I really, really hate except for microwave burgers or squirty cream and I was pretty certain they wouldn't be on the menu. More to the point, he was wearing his chef's jacket and that always made me extra-susceptible (it's the only uniform I've ever found a turn-on).

Callum slipped a velvet blindfold over my eyes and I heard him pottering around the kitchen, then it all went quiet. The next thing I knew, he was saying, 'Open wide.' I did as I was told and felt something cold and fizzy spill over my tongue. He was 'feeding' me champagne.

I swallowed and he asked me, 'Are you ready for your *amuse bouche*?' I nodded, feeling oddly submissive. This wasn't just about appreciating the flavours; there was something else going on too. He pushed a Chinese spoon into my mouth and I tasted the most incredible soup I'd ever had. It was some kind of fish – lobster, I later found out – and the flavours were really intense. There was also a sensation of pearls bursting in my mouth, which he told me was smoked salmon roe.

Next up, he fed me a single scallop marinated in ginger, then a piece of raw beef that he'd coated with a really spicy chilli rub and sliced thinly. He spooned a mouthful of grapefruit granita into my mouth before making me lean my head back as he poured a rich game stew down my throat. He followed that with a dumpling that he'd simmered in the stew, so the flavour was amazing. By the time it got to dessert – a perfect crème brûlée with fresh berries – my head was spinning from the flavours. But the best bit of dessert was yet to come.

Without removing my blindfold, Callum rubbed his cock against my lips. It was covered with an intense strawberry sauce and I couldn't resist licking it. Before long, I had cream to go with my strawberries . . . . But the night was far from over.

After he'd come, Callum took the blindfold off and kissed me passionately. Then he stripped me and poured the strawberry sauce all over my body and slowly licked it off. He was so reverential, I felt like I was the most exquisite delicacy he'd ever tasted. He wouldn't let me come, but kept me hovering on the edge of orgasm for over an hour. When he eventually slid inside me, I came after just a few thrusts and he came shortly afterwards. The build-up had been so intense that I was shaking for about half an hour afterwards.

Needless to say, when he next invited me to dinner, I said yes. The rest is history. We're getting married next year, and I've already told him that I want us to have a special wedding breakfast all on our own . . .

Sally, 31, antique dealer

Food Fight

Another way to enjoy food fun is with a good old-fashioned food fight. This is wasteful though, so make sure you choose foods that go a long way: for example, packet desserts like Angel Delight, own-brand cartons of custard poured on to paper plates and topped with whipped cream from a can or cheap packet cake mix made up with water.

If possible, use the garden for your food fight so that you can go really wild, then simply hose down the area afterwards. You could set up trestle tables at either end of the garden with equal amounts of custard pies, bowls of cake mix and cartons of custard, put on your oldest and tattiest clothes (or cheap swimsuits), then, on an agreed signal, let the fighting begin. Afterwards, you can either enjoy having messy sex together on a plastic sheet in the garden (but be warned: you'll slide around a lot) or hose each other down to get the worst of the mess off your clothes then retire to the bathroom to share a sexy shower. You could also agree that the 'loser' has to give the 'winner' a sexual reward to add an extra thrill to proceedings and give you both that fighting spirit.

If you don't have a garden, you can either use the bathroom (but make sure you put down plastic sheeting if you have a carpeted rather than tiled floor) or opt for a night in a hotel so that someone else has to deal with the mess . . .

TRUE CONFESSIONS
IT WAS STICKY FUN

Ever since I saw the film *Tom Jones* I've liked the idea of having a food fight, and when I mentioned the idea to my fiancé after the film had been on TV one night, he was totally up for it: he's a big kid at heart. We decided that our best bet was to go to a hotel room with a big bathroom so we didn't mess up our house, though what they must have thought of us taking three big bags of supermarket shopping in with us for a one-night stay, I don't know.

When we got into the room, we were both giggling. Although the idea was sexy it did seem a little silly, particularly when we were setting up a platter of chicken drumsticks in the bathroom!

Although it felt a little contrived at first, taking bites out of drumsticks and hurling them behind us, then pushing asparagus dipped in hollandaise into each other's faces, when he hit a chocolate cake right in my face, I saw red and started ripping chunks out of a pavlova and throwing it at him. Next came the chocolate sauce which looked disgusting smeared all over his face, but gave me a great feeling of satisfaction. We ended up slipping onto the floor (I had bruises all over me afterwards but it was worth it) and had sex in the middle of all of the mess.

Afterwards, we did our best to clean it up but all the towels ended up covered in chocolate sauce. I don't know what the maid must have thought when she found them all but we left a big tip, so I'm hoping she didn't hate us too much. It's definitely something that I'd try again; it felt so naughty throwing food at each other, and I had a great sense of triumph when I managed to get my boyfriend with two pieces of lemon meringue pie – one over each ear – at the same time. His revenge afterwards was a lot of fun as well . . .

Caramel, 27, librarian

Custard Wrestling

If messy sex really rings your bell, you could take things even further by entering into a sploshing session and filling a paddling pool with custard, cake mix or some other similarly gloopy substance, then getting into it with your partner and having a wrestle. Again, you could reward your partner with a sexual treat every time they manage to 'pin' you, and earn sexual pleasures of your own by pinning them. Afterwards, you can either enjoy each other while you're still covered in custard or have a bath together and get clean – before getting dirty all over again.

EMILY'S EXPERIENCES: I WRESTLED A STRANGER IN CUSTARD

One of the assignments that I least looked forward to was sploshing. Even though Bill, the guy who runs Splosh Studios and is pretty much responsible for creating the genre, seemed lovely via email, the idea of getting covered in cake mix, custard, eggs and baked beans was something that didn't really appeal. Particularly the eggs and baked beans. Maybe it was growing up in the days of the salmonella outbreak, but the idea of having raw eggs squished against me filled me with disgust. Still, as Bill had been running the studio for years I figured it was OK to tell him my reservations. He was totally understanding, and agreed that I could have a strictly 'sweet' sploshing experience.

Come the day, I arrived at Splosh Studios (basically, a garage with lots of plastic sheeting around, plus the all-important shower to get clean afterwards) and was introduced to my 'partner in crime', the lovely and voluptuous Decadent Dolly. A full-time splosh model and performer, she told me there was nothing to worry about and said she'd go gently on me. Soon, we were chatting like old friends and Bill announced that it was time for us to start.

I'd deliberately worn a PVC full-length ball dress to avoid 'clothes going see-through' issues; wrestling in custard is one thing but showing my bits in a national magazine quite another. A table to one side of us was covered in pre-prepared custard pies, bowls of cake mix, squeezy bottles of maple-syrup-flavoured ice-cream topping and cartons of custard ready for us to pour all over each other. The floor was covered in a tarpaulin to protect it from getting too messy – unlike us!

When the first custard pie hit me, I was surprised to find that it was really cold. But the shock of the impact was nothing compared to the sense of outrage that rose up in me, making me want to do nothing more than to pile a custard pie into Dolly's face, along with an incredible urge to giggle.

I grabbed a pie and aimed it at Dolly's face, not quite getting her full on but causing cream and custard to trickle down the side of her face. After that, it was war. We poured custard over each other, threw handfuls of cake mixture and used the squeezy ice-cream-topping bottles as makeshift guns to drench each other with sticky sauce. Even though I didn't find it arousing, it was really good fun, but as the fight progressed, I discovered that it gets very slippery when you're hurling food around the place, and we were soon writhing around on the floor like lesbians in a mud-bath movie.

We seemed to run out of 'ingredients' in no time, at which point Bill called a halt to the proceedings and we went to shower ourselves off. I scrubbed myself for ages to get the sticky gunk out of my hair and off my dress, but I could still smell maple syrup inside my nose all the way home, and it took about four days for my hair to recover from all the custard that had been liberally applied to it: cornflour is not a good hair conditioner.

Overall, I'm glad that I had a go at sploshing, and it's certainly something I'd recommend everyone tries at least once, if only for the sense of exhilaration that playing with your food (such a childhood taboo) can bring. Treat it with a sense of humour and you'll have a fantastic time. Just make sure you have someone else to clean up the mess!

Figging

While food play is generally fairly sensual (or silly), there are some practices that use food to administer pain rather than pleasure: specifically, figging. The name figging has nothing to do with the fruit, but comes from an old practice known as 'feaguing', in which horse dealers would insert ginger into a horse's rectum. The horse would react to the sensation caused by the ginger by holding its tail high and moving around nervously – behaviour which is more characteristic of a younger horse. The sexual kink of figging entails peeling a root of ginger, carving it into a butt-plug shape to stop it from getting stuck, then inserting it into the rectum. The ginger juice causes extreme pain and tightens up the anal sphincter. Ginger can also be used to cause similar levels of pain to the vagina or clitoris and, if either the vagina or anus is clenched while the ginger is in place, the pain will be intensified.

If you're curious about trying figging, but the idea of too much pain intimidates you, it's possible to emulate it at a milder level by rubbing a small amount of ginger juice on to a butt plug or dildo. Using lubricant to help the ginger into place will also decrease the pain, as it coats the root. (If you're not using lubricant, you should be extra careful to go slowly and relax your partner before you slide the ginger into them, otherwise you could cause small cuts to the anus which will intensify the pain to scary levels. Use water to give it at least a small amount of lubrication.)

Should you decide that figging is just too mild for you (and trust me, it's unlikely, unless you're seriously into pain), an even crueller alternative to ginger is chilli. However, this can cause extreme irritation (hell, the ginger root option isn't exactly a walk in the park), so is best avoided unless really severe pain gets you off, and it should be done entirely at your own risk.

TRUE CONFESSIONS

MY BOYFRIEND LOVES PAIN, SO I GAVE IT TO HIM

I'm a dominant woman and was lucky enough to meet my perfect 'sub' a few years ago. He likes me to push his limits, so when I read about figging in a newsgroup, I decided to give it a go. I tied him up and blindfolded him (he loves being out of control), then told him that he had to follow my orders precisely. I took the ginger that I'd already peeled and held it under his nose. 'Sniff it,' I ordered. He did as he was told and I asked him to guess what it was. He got it wrong a couple of times, for which he got a couple of hits with my crop, then finally got it right. I asked him what he thought I was going to use it for and he wouldn't say at first (for which he took more punishment), but eventually said, 'Figging?' He'd been with me when I'd seen the post on the forum, so I'm guessing he'd been waiting for me to suggest it – he knows that's how I get my evil ideas most of the time.

'Spot on,' I told him, and proceeded to slide it inside him. He wriggled around and moaned, which is something he's banned from doing and usually very good about, so I knew that it was really hurting him, which just turned me on more. When the base of the ginger butt plug finally rested against his perineum, I told him that it was all the way in and I saw him start to relax, although he was still wriggling. I ordered him to be still but he kept moving, so I told him he'd have to clench his muscles by way of apology, otherwise it was staying in there all night.

When he followed my order he almost screamed (if the look on his face was anything to go by), but he held it back, so I told him he was a good boy and slipped it out a few seconds later. We haven't tried it again – he said it was too much for him; but I often threaten him with a figging session if I'm feeling particularly nasty and make sure I've always got ginger in the house now, just in case he's disobedient . . .

Alexandra, 37, self-described Domme

Vore-play

At a similarly extreme end of the food play fetish, albeit more psychological than physical, is vore. Named after the Latin word for swallow' or 'devour', vore fetishists like to imagine eating a lover, being eaten or watching the process. However, this doesn't mean that they are actually cannibals in any way. Instead, vore fetishists simply use genuine props and condiments to play out their fantasy.

There are various vore scenarios. One of the classics is hog-tying a partner to a spit, then basting them and sticking an apple in their mouth, as if they are a suckling pig. This is a deeply submissive position to be in, as the 'pig' can neither speak nor escape. While people may enjoy being turned on a spit, it should go without saying that there's no actual fire underneath it! You should also ensure that you only suspend someone if you've had a training course in suspension bondage, otherwise you can cause major damage to their back or even throttle them. A safer option is to hog-tie your partner on the floor. You can either use a rope harness (*see* p. 212) or simply tie your partner's ankles and wrists together behind their back.

But hog-tying isn't the only option. Some of the more serious vore fetishists have giant frying pans, fake stoves or even microwave ovens that they put their 'food' into. If the idea appeals to you, you can always hire oversized props from theatrical companies (they are easy to find online); just make sure that you clean the props thoroughly after use, so nobody knows what you've been up to.

While vore may sound rather extreme, the standard cannibalism fetish has many more traditionally sexual aspects to it than it may at first appear. For example, the 'victim' is often 'captured', stripped, tied up, oiled up, taunted and poked, all of which takes a lot from classic submissive fantasies with some bondage and massage thrown in for good measure. And vore is as much about the imagination as it is about the actual act (as is the case with many fetishes), which is why it is far more psychological than physical. Indeed, many practitioners say that the main kick comes from feeling so desirable that their lover must consume them in every way, which is something it's easy to empathise with.

One of the advantages of vore-play is that you can get pretty much everything you need to test it out at a standard cook shop or supermarket: olive oil, pastry and basting brushes, turkey basters and meat forks will all help you get into the mood. (You can file the ends off the meat forks to stop them from actually causing any damage.) Do be careful about using herbs or any other form of stuffing in intimate places, though: it's a sure-fire way to get yeast infections, and you don't want anything getting stuck (unless, that is, the idea of an embarrassing trip to casualty turns you on).

'The cannibals make me feel like a goddess. They like my rounded belly and the little pockets of fat at the tops of my thighs. These are things that the mainstream erotica industry tends to frown upon, but in the cannibal world they're celebrated.'

Megh, vore fetishist, as quoted in *Scarlet* magazine

If all of this sounds far too contrived for you, but the idea of dabbling with vore appeals, a simpler option is to just talk dirty to your partner about vore while they're blindfolded in a hot bath. That way, they can pretend that they're simmering away ready to be consumed by you, but you don't need to worry about a host of props. Well, sometimes a supermarket trip is just too much hassle.

Are You Ready For More?

So, now you've thoroughly explored the contents of your kitchen cupboard (and possibly your local cook shop) you will have begun to discover the effect that incorporating props into your sex life can have. Maybe you've turned your lover into a sexy dessert, perhaps you've discovered to joys of messy sex or you may have simply decided to incorporate a sensual meal into your dating schedule each week.

If you're feeling sated, then leave it there. But if you want to feed your fetish side some more, get ready for the next chapter, in which you'll learn about the many other kinky props and costumes you can incorporate into your sex life. From dildos and sex furniture to corsets and thigh boots, there's all manner of stuff out there that can change the way you have sex. And hell, there's no reason why you should stick to just one prop at a time . . .

CHAPTER FOUR

Kinky Props and Fetish Fashion

Food play is all very well, but once you've started to incorporate extras into your sex life, you may decide that you'd also like to experiment with props that are specifically designed for sex, rather than any that are already in your fridge. And it'll probably come as no surprise to you to learn that there's a vast number of kink aids to work your way through. That said, it can still be intimidating to walk into a fetish shop and see exactly how much scope you've got for play, particularly if you try figuring out what some of the strange devices in the display cabinets actually do. Trust me, there are some things out there that even I've had to ask about – and that's after nearly a decade testing sex toys.

At the mildest end of the spectrum, there are all manner of dildos and butt plugs, vibrators and love eggs, strap-ons and nipple teasers. You can get toys in all shapes and sizes, designed to stimulate a woman's clitoris, G-spot and anus or a man's shaft, balls, perineum and prostate, or sometimes a combination of the above. And they come in all different types of material: vinyl, silicone, wood, crystal, rubber, PVC and even precious metals complete with gem trim. No matter what sort of stimulation you're looking for, it's almost guaranteed that there's a toy out there to do the job. However, it can be hard to navigate your way through the various options if you're not sure exactly what you're after, particularly if you have to bear a partner's feelings in mind at the same time.

And sex toys aren't the only props that you can involve in your bedroom antics. You can also get furniture designed to make sex positions you'd always thought impossible an absolute doddle, or simply to make your favourite positions even more effective. Foam wedges, sex swings and even sheets with instructions as to how to get into specific sex positions can all help you to get a lot more creative than your normal household furniture does. (Then again, don't underestimate how much fun you can have on a sofa, kitchen table or washing machine . . .)

Then there's dressing up; the right outfit can make all the difference to sex. In addition to the role-play outfits covered in Chapter One, some couples find that adding a pair of stiletto heels or thigh-high boots to the equation gives sex an extra kick. Even something as simple as seeing a partner wearing stockings, tights, an ankle bracelet or nail varnish on perfectly manicured feet can be thrilling for some people. And that's before you've even thought about the whole PVC, rubber and leather scene, which offers numerous options to explore.

'Everyone advertises themselves with what they wear. Fetish wear does exactly that in a very visible way.'
Ashley Hames, TV presenter and sexual explorer

Should you decide to dabble with fetish fashion, one of the more intense experiences available is wearing a corset. While some people simply enjoy the way that a corset makes them look, others get off on the constriction and choose to train their waists down to ridiculously tiny levels – 17 inches (43cm) or smaller.

In a similar vein, you might choose to indulge in pony play, in which you're trussed up with harnesses, blinkers and reins, and have to lead your partner around in their very own carriage. If you're more of a dog person, you might opt for puppy play instead, in which you wear a collar and leash and are treated like a canine; while cat people needn't miss out, because kitten play is another kinky option.

And if that little lot still isn't quite hardcore enough for you, there's the whole realm of sexual piercings to work your way through, whether in the nipples, clitoris, penis or elsewhere. While this isn't always about getting a sexual thrill, there are certainly ways in which piercings can enhance your sex life (as long as you make sure that you get them at a reputable piercing salon: infected piercings are the last thing you want when you're feeling horny).

But before we get into that, let's start at the mildest end of the scale: sexy lingerie. Getting dressed up for your partner is one of the easiest ways to show them that you're in the mood for lust. And there are so many fun ways to incorporate it into your sex life that it's one of the best places to start.

Let Me Slip into Something More Comfortable

Sexy lingerie has long been a fixture in adult magazines, and it's no big surprise that most men find a woman in stockings and suspenders, frilly knickers or a shows-more-than-it-hides thong a turn-on. After all, it indicates not only that the woman is up for sex, but that she's put some thought into it too. For some men, just the idea that a woman has considered sex can be a turn-on, before you even get into the way that she looks.

But obviously lingerie is designed to flatter your assets too (as long as you choose the right items – crotchless panties are good for no woman, unless her partner has a fetish for them). Stockings and suspenders give an enticing glimpse of upper thigh that just yearns to be kissed. Push-up bras do a similar job for breasts. And thongs draw attention to the buttocks, which are a key sexual signifier, dating from the time that we crawled around on all fours (prehistorically, that is, rather than the last time you got wasted) so that buttocks, not breasts, were a major way to attract a mate. As such, any of these items is likely to drive a man wild. Wearing lingerie also has a wonder-ful air of the tease about it. Although a woman is on display, she also has to be 'unwrapped', which can add a whole new level of anticipation to sex.

And it's not just women that can wear sexy undies. Calvin Klein pants are ideal for flattering a man's package, and there are other more niche items, including: pants with a padded bum (to enhance the male derrière), trunks with a padded crotch (to enhance his package; although wearing one may cause a woman to cite the Trade Descriptions Act); and even the Ball Bra, which cups the balls but leaves the penis free, should you have an issue with the sensation of balls slapping against your bits during sex. (No, I don't entirely understand why such a thing exists either, and the numerous kinky friends I've shown it to are similarly clueless. Still, it takes all sorts.)

Buying your partner sexy lingerie shows that you've been thinking erotic thoughts about them which can be a turn-on in itself. However, it's very easy to make mistakes, particularly when it comes to buying lingerie for women. As a general guideline, you're safest sticking with cream, white or black underwear, unless you know that your partner has a penchant for a particular colour. Red is certainly best avoided as it's a case of finding exactly the right red, which is no mean feat. I used to work in a lingerie store as a student. On Christmas Eve, men would buy up every item of red underwear in the shop. On Boxing Day, women would return it, which just goes to show how tricky it is to get right. You should also make damned sure that you get it in the right size. By far the easiest way to do this, regardless of your partner's gender, is to check the label on the inside of some underwear that you know they wear on a regular basis. If you haven't had a chance to do this and are buying an emergency present, the safest bet for men is to overestimate the top half (unless your partner is paranoid about her breasts being too big) and underestimate the bottom half (trust me, no woman will object if you think her bum is smaller than it actually is). And for women, always go larger: you can always say that you were worried your man's package wouldn't fit into small or medium pants.

Don't pick something in a totally different style from your partner's usual underwear either. There's probably a good reason why they stick to a given look; particular styles of underwear suit certain body shapes and your lover may well opt for something that hides parts of their body they dislike. So if you're not going shopping together, err on the side of caution. However, it's certainly well worth considering a mutual underwear shopping jaunt as this can be a form of foreplay all of its own.

TRUE CONFESSIONS

I FELT LIKE I WAS IN *PRETTY WOMAN*

A few years ago I dated a guy called Tim, who was much richer than my usual boyfriends. I was a poor student, so was more used to having half a cider and sharing a kebab than getting whizzed around town in a sports car and drinking cocktails in fancy bars. Tim was a few years older than me and used to joke about being my sugar daddy, even though he was only in his twenties. One day, he commented that I didn't have any matching underwear. 'You buy it for me, I'll wear it for you,' I joked. 'OK then,' he replied. 'Let's go.'

I objected at first. I didn't feel comfortable with him buying me presents, as I couldn't reciprocate. But he insisted that he'd get as much pleasure out of it as I would, so eventually, I agreed.

He took me to a small boutique in the centre of town. Everything there was clearly very expensive, but he banned me from looking at any of the price tags and told me to pick anything that I liked the look of. I picked things that looked like they'd cost the least amount of money, so he started pulling things from the shelves for me, saying that if I wouldn't pick what I really wanted, he'd have to help. His domineering tone was quite sexy, as was the idea of being bought lots of expensive underwear, 'whether I liked it or not', if I'm really honest. So I let him carry on choosing things before he led me through to the changing rooms.

I'd been expecting a communal changing room as I'd only ever been into high-street stores before, so when I saw the peep-show-style booth with elegant red curtains, I was taken aback. Tim said that he could wait outside if I wanted, but that the changing rooms were designed so that you could watch your lover getting changed. It seemed like such a sexy idea, so I told him to wait for a few seconds so I could get undressed (I wanted him to see me slipping into sexy undies, not taking off my old unsexy ones!) and then come through.

Inside the booth, I realised that I needn't have worried as there was a cover for the peephole on my side, meaning I could decide when I wanted him to look at me by lifting it up. I shrugged my clothes off and laced up a sexy corset that I teamed with a pair of black French knickers. When I lifted the peephole, I could tell he was impressed. He asked me to give him a twirl, which I did. Then I decided that playing the stripper would be sexy, so I teasingly undressed, gave him a quick flash, then closed the peephole again. I worked my way through five different outfits in this way. Each time, he asked me to do a twirl for him, and I have to admit to feeling very turned on by the time I got out the changing room.

Once I'd tried all the outfits on, Tim told me to go to the cocktail bar opposite and he'd buy the things that he liked me in best. When he walked in with three big bags, I realised he'd bought me everything! I felt like a princess, or Julia Roberts in *Pretty Woman* (but without the hooker inference). On the way home he told me all the things he'd wanted to do to me when I was in the changing room, which made me feel even more turned on. Needless to say, he got a fashion show when we got home and got to do everything he'd wanted to and more.

Even though we split up about six months later, I still
have fond memories of that afternoon. And I've still got
all the underwear too!

Alicia, 25, researcher

Hairs and graces

The right underwear will certainly show you off in your best
light, but it's worth putting some effort into what lies beneath
as well. Although you can leave things au naturel, nowadays an
increasing number of women are choosing to groom their
pubic hair in some way. At the most basic level, you can trim
your pubes back to stop them from getting in the way during
oral sex, or leave a neat triangle of hair over your pubic mound
but defoliate the outer labia to make things even easier. At a
wilder level, you can shape your pubic hair into a heart or light-
ening bolt, dye it bright pink, shave the whole lot off or go one
step further and trim your shaved mons with diamante stickers.
And men are increasingly getting in on the act too, albeit at a
lower level, by either trimming their pubic hair or shaving it off
altogether, having realised that it makes the penis look bigger.
(This is why the majority of men in porn remove all body hair
down below.)

However, before you go mad with the razor, it is worth bearing in mind that some people find copious amounts of body
hair a turn-on, so make sure that you check with your partner
first. It could be that what they'd really like is for you to grow
your armpit hair and leg hair to match a 1970s-style muff, and
the idea of being confronted with a hairless haven is the biggest
possible turn-off.

TRUE CONFESSIONS
THE BRAZILIAN SHOULD BE BANNED

I hit my teens in the 1970s when women in porn magazines (which I saw only when I was lucky enough to find
pages in hedges, being far too shy to actually buy a magazine for myself) looked like real women. They had this
vibrant, springy hair between their legs and it was so forbidden, so tempting to touch, so damned furry, that all I
needed to do was see a glimpse of muff and I'd be hard.
(Then again, when I sat on the bus I'd get hard; it wasn't
a rare occurrence – I was a sixteen-year-old boy.)

I got married in my twenties, so porn was something
that moved to the back burner because my wife didn't
approve. Of course, I saw the odd film when I went
round to see one of my friends who had a pretty good
old-school video collection, but it wasn't really a major
part of my life.

My wife and I divorced a couple of years ago and,
understandably, porn was back on the cards. I bought a
magazine rather than searching the local hedges, but I was
turned off rather than turned on: all the hair had been
removed and the women in the magazines looked like
teenagers rather than anything I could find arousing. The
fully shaved ones were the worst – it looked all pink and
sore – but even those that did have hair had trimmed it
back so it looked more like a Hitler moustache than a real
woman's pubes. I don't find Hitler a turn-on.

After searching the Internet, I was relieved to find that
it is still possible to find decent porn, where women look
like women rather than plucked turkeys (even if I do have

to type in 'hairy women' to find them, which is something I find ridiculous). I can't understand why pubes became unfashionable. Pubic hair is a sign that a woman has reached maturity, and seeing someone who's removed it is about as appealing as chatting up a girl who's in school uniform (something else I've never seen the appeal of; give me a fully grown woman rather than an immature girl any day of the week). Whatever happened to the glorious abundance of a natural woman with a full bush?

Andrew, 49, salesman

If you do decide to enter into the world of body-hair removal, there are a few things that will make the whole experience better. To start with, trim your hair before you shave or depilate it. (Under no circumstances should you consider using an epilator on your pubic area unless you're seriously into pain.) This way you're less likely to blunt the razor and end up chafing your skin. Then, if you're opting for the shaving route:

- **Use warm water rather than hot.** This dries the skin less, so will minimise itchy grow-back.

- **Oil or foam?** Some people swear by shaving oil, while others say that foam is best, but whichever you choose, make sure you keep it away from the mucous membranes (wet bits) so that you don't suffer from any irritation. It's also best to use an oil or foam that's formulated for sensitive skin.

- **Shave with the direction of hair growth rather than against it.** Do this for minimal irritation, and make sure that you cover your clit with your finger when you're nearing it, or pull your balls down to tighten the skin sac: the last thing you want is to nick these sensitive areas.

- **Rinse all the shaving foam or oil off thoroughly.** Then splash with cold water to close the pores (don't even think about using aftershave, as it will sting like hell and can cause irritation if you get it anywhere intimate).

- **Moisturise thoroughly.** Use a sensitive-skin moisturiser or, better yet, nappy-rash cream. Continue to moisturise every day and you'll minimise itchy grow-back.

Obviously, you can incorporate shaving each other into foreplay but you need to be extra careful if you do so: imagine the row you'll end up having if you inadvertently nick your partner's bits when you're shaving them. And this definitely isn't something to try when you're drunk, no matter how sexy the idea may seem.

As an alternative way to remove your pubes, you could choose to use a depilatory cream. If you go for this option, make sure that you only use one that's specifically designed for the pubic area and be very, very careful not to get it on the mucous membranes. If you want to shape your pubes, depilatory cream offers the easiest DIY option. Simply cut a paper template of whatever shape you want (a heart is easy as you just fold the paper in half to cut out a perfectly even shape, as is a Christmas tree if you're feeling festive), then use sticky tape to fix it to your pubic hair and apply the depilatory cream around the edges of the template. Leave it on for the recommended time (never longer, especially in the pubic area, as you can cause serious damage to your skin).

Once the cream has had time to work its magic, simply rinse it off and voilà, you have a perfectly shaped bush. (**Note:** make sure that you depilate any hairs around your anus too – anal beard is not a good look. However, don't get any cream on the anus itself as it can cause irritation.) It should go without saying that using a depilatory cream is best performed when you're alone as there's no way to look dignified when you're standing John Wayne-style with cream all over your bush and anal area, not to mention that the cream rarely smells pleasant.

Another option is to get a professional beautician to wax your hair away. This has the advantage of lasting longer than either shaving or using depilatory cream. However, it's strongly recommended that you take a painkiller an hour before you are waxed, otherwise it'll really make your eyes water (rather than just hurt like hell)! And don't be surprised if you end up getting in-growing hairs; waxing is the worst of all the pubic-removal methods in this respect. You can minimise the chances of this happening by using an exfoliating glove on the area once the initial redness has died down. Check with your beautician to see how quickly they think it will be safe to do this, as different waxing methods take different amounts of recovery time. And never get your bits waxed on the same day as you're planning a naughty night. Screaming, 'Don't touch me, it stings,' is hardly a libido booster (unless you're into the whole sub/Dom thing).

Of course, shaving or shaping your pubes is only the beginning when it comes to getting kinky. Once you've got everything styled to perfection, you'll probably want to show it off. And what could be better than putting on a toy show, so that your lover can admire your bits in all their glory? But first of all, you need to make sure that you've got the toys.

Toys for Grown-ups

Nowadays, sex toys have entered the mainstream enough that they may not seem fetishistic at all to some people. However, there are still many couples who consider the idea of getting plastic fantastic to be most definitely kinky. And if you think about it, sex toys fit into the technical definition of a fetish because you're attaching sexual significance to something that is 'an object or non-genital part of the body that causes a habitual erotic response or fixation' (even if said object was designed with sexual pleasure in mind). So it's certainly something that fits into the 'friendly fetish' world.

While some toys are clearly designed to look like the genitals that they're emulating, you can now get vibrators in the shape of a cone or sphere, a lipstick, a bath sponge and numerous different colours of rubber duck. There's even a butt-plug in the shape of George Bush (but you'd need to be pretty damned kinky to find the idea of George Bush in your nether regions a turn-on). At the more standard end of the range are numerous variations of the 'Rabbit' – a vibrator with a rotating shaft to stimulate the G-spot and 'bunny ears' to rub against the clitoris – along with small 'bullets' that tend to deliver more intense vibrations, love eggs and traditional 'non-doctor' vibrators that look like a smooth plastic version of a penis, to name just a few.

And sex toys aren't just for women. The last few years have seen a massive extension in the range of sex toys for men. In addition to the somewhat risible inflatable dolls on the market, you can now get ribbed, ridged or 'bobbled' masturbation gloves that either partner wears to give a different sensation when masturbating the penis. There are suction cups designed to simulate oral sex, fake vaginas and anuses (sometimes both at once) that come in a handy can for ease of storage and prostate massagers should a man prefer stimulation where the sun doesn't shine. If you're really loaded, there's even the option to get sex dolls that look exactly like real women (and can be modelled, somewhat creepily, on a partner of your choice, whether it's your actual partner or a total stranger). While women may not have quite the same desire to watch their partner using a toy as men tend to, the range of options available means that, should you want to, the resultant show won't make your partner collapse in giggles. (As long as you don't opt for the doll.)

While some people are uncomfortable with the idea of using sex toys (or, just as commonly, feel intimidated at the idea of their partner using them), they can be a fabulous way to add extra fun to your sex sessions and they're a lot less expensive nowadays than you might think. In most countries, you can get one of the very cheapest sex toys for as little as the cost of a bottle of beer, although there are also designer sex toys made from platinum trimmed with diamonds, which will, of course, set you back a lot more. Basically, there are toys to suit every budget, so being broke needn't be a barrier to getting into toy play.

If you do like the idea of experimenting with toys, don't just plunge in by presenting your lover with a bag full of vibrators or masturbation sheaths, a multi-pack of batteries and a jumbo bottle of lube. While this may work for some couples, there's still a stigma attached to the idea of masturbation for many people, particularly if it's their partner doing it. They may fear that a sex toy is a replacement for actual sex, or a negative comment about their sexual technique. They might worry that a partner could become addicted to sex toys and go off penetrative sex or they could be concerned that a toy is bigger or tighter than they are and, as such, will increase a partner's expectations to unrealistic measures. Or they might just feel foolish about the idea of using a piece of plastic to get off.

Before you even consider spending any money on a toy, it's worth discussing any concerns and expectations that you may have about incorporating toys into the relationship. If one partner is reticent, don't push the issue; there's no point trying something new unless both of you are into the idea. However, there really is no need to feel intimidated by a toy. It may be available and willing all the time (assuming you've got enough batteries), but it can't give you a hug or a compliment, it can't kiss and it can't make you a cup of tea after sex, so there's no way it's remotely comparable to a real-life partner. (OK, not all partners will do all the above either, but at least they can be trained.)

There are many ways in which sex toys can help to improve your sex life. If one of you feels frisky and the other one isn't in the mood, a toy can help relieve the pressure. If one of you has reached climax during sex and just wants to go to sleep, a toy can help you give your partner an orgasm before you doze off, and thus stop you from being perceived as a lazy lover. Obviously, having toys in the house makes it more likely that you can fit in a quickie masturbation session when you get a spare five minutes, which can only be a positive thing because orgasms are good for your health as well as feeling pretty damned amazing. And this isn't just good for *you* either: according to research, the more orgasms a person has, the more they want, so you're actually more likely rather than less so to pounce on your partner if you masturbate on a regular basis.

EMILY'S EXPERIENCES: *TESTING TIMES*

When I'm testing toys for the *Scarlet* reviews page, I do them all on the same day – that way, I can ensure that my libido is at the same level for all of them, rather than letting my hormones dictate how effective I'll find a toy. As such, I'll have at least four toys to try out in one day. When I first met my partner he assumed that toy-testing day would be a time when he'd have to sort himself out because I'd be sated from work. In actual fact, the opposite is true. After an hour or so of testing toys, I find myself craving the real thing: a vibrator is all very well, but a good sex session is so much better. The only downside is that he has to wait until I've got all my reviews out of the way first: work is work, after all.

Once you've discussed any concerns that you might have about sex toys, by far the easiest way to introduce them into your relationship is to buy a toy together that you can *use* together. That way, you can ensure that neither of you feels uncomfortable with the toy, either mentally or physically, and both of you get maximum benefit from it.

There are numerous ways in which to use sex toys together. For example, a bullet-style vibrator can be held against the clitoris during sex to increase a woman's pleasure, or held against the perineum during penetrative or oral sex to increase the man's. A vibrating cock ring will help a man stay harder for longer while increasing the thrills for his partner. And anal beads can be used by either partner to add an extra dimension to sex (but don't share them, unless you wash them thoroughly and use anti-bacterial wipes on them in between sessions).

You can also get toys that are specifically designed for couples: cock ring/bullet vibe combinations that are attached to each other so you can use both at once; finger vibrators that either partner can slip on to add an extra buzz to manual stimulation; and oral sex toys that either slip over the tongue or through a tongue-piercing hole, if you have one, and vibrate as your tongue works its magic.

And toys don't just have to be used when you're together in a physical sense. You can now get vibrators powered by mobile phone calls: send your lover a text message and, if the toy is in place, you'll give them an extra thrill. There are remote-controlled vibrators that are discreet enough to wear in public and a fantastic way to get your partner's attention when they're on the other side of the room at a party. And there are vibrators that connect to your computer and can be controlled by a lover across the Internet, so you can still indulge in toy play even when you're apart.

Of course, sex toys don't just have to be about the obvious erogenous zones. Blindfolds can be used for sensual play as well as more extreme kink, and feather ticklers, fake-fur mitts and satin gloves can all be used to change the sensation of stroking your partner's skin.

And then there are the numerous lotions and potions that are out there. You can now get creams to tighten the vagina or swell the G-spot, intensify stimulation or delay ejaculation and warm on contact to give a new sensation altogether. However, do be careful when using such creams: test them on your inner thigh and wait for twenty-four hours before applying them anywhere more sensitive, as you don't want to discover an allergy by getting bumps all over your bits. That said, as long as you buy these products from a reputable supplier you should be fine; it's just better to be safe than sorry when it comes to genital health.

If you're still not sure what to buy when you hit the sex shop or online store, think about the ways that you most like to be stimulated, then pick a toy designed for the purpose. See it as an addition to your sex life rather than a replacement: what's the harm in having an extra way to bring your partner pleasure, after all?

Clitoral stimulation

This is by far the most common sort of stimulation that women seek, and every vibrator will provide it as long as you, surprise, surprise, hold it against the clitoris. However, not all toys are created equal. The ubiquitous Rabbit has specially designed bunny ears that press against the clitoris and vibrate separately from the shaft which probably explains why it's one of the bestselling toys on the market. Indeed, many women only use the bunny ears and don't actually insert the shaft inside themselves at all (although if you do, and turn on the vibrate function, it'll provide G-spot stimulation at the same time, which is certainly an experience that every woman should try at least once).

But the rabbit is less than ideal if you want to use a vibrator on your clitoris during sex to speed your orgasm, so if that's what you're after, opt for a bullet-type toy. Do check the level of vibrations before purchase if you possibly can, though. If you're new to toys, a mild buzz is probably best to start with (unless you find it hard to climax because you don't have a particularly sensitive clitoris), as the sensation does take a little getting used to. Should you inadvertently buy a toy that's too intense for you, however, don't panic. You can lessen the vibrations, either by using a battery that's near the end of its life or by putting your hand between the vibrator and your bits. Generally speaking, the harder the toy, the more intense the vibrations, so a 'real-feel cyberskin' toy will be a lot gentler than a hard plastic vibe. And use your common sense when it comes to picking a toy to use during sex: a smaller, flatter toy will obviously be much easier to hold against yourself than a massive vibrating phallus.

G-spot stimulation

While some people claim that the G-spot is a myth, hundreds of thousands of women would claim that this is nonsense. Just a few inches inside the vagina on the upper wall, the G-spot is an area that swells when stimulated and is thought to be the top of the clitoris (which is wishbone shaped and actually extends inside the vagina; the thing that we identify as the clitoris is actually just the tip). The swelling is caused by a build-up of prostatic fluid (basically, semen without the sperm in it) and if the G-spot is stimulated in the right way, this fluid can be released causing female ejaculation. If you do squirt when your G-spot is stimulated, don't panic, it's not urine (even though some women feel as if they want to urinate when their G-spot is stimulated as it's so close to the bladder), but you can still end up with a hefty wet patch.

You have several options when it comes to G-spot stimulation with toys. The first is to opt for a vibrator or dildo that has a curved tip. This can be positioned, with the curve pointing upwards, to press against the upper wall of the vagina and hit the elusive spot. You can get toys of different girths, but it may be easiest to start with one of the more slender models on the market. It can take a while to find the spot and you might want to practise alone first so that you can guide your partner to the right place, but once you find it, you may well find that it enhances your orgasm, so it's certainly worth the hunt.

Another option is simply to opt for a very large toy. This isn't recommended if you have a partner with penis-size issues, as they'll only end up feeling inadequate. You should also ensure that you use a lot of lubricant with large toys as it's entirely possibly to give yourself cystitis if you use something that's too big for you. However, one of the advantages of a large toy is that it's damned near impossible to miss your G-spot, so you won't have to faff around, angling it in the right way.

EMILY'S EXPERIENCES: I GAVE MYSELF HONEYMOON CYSTITIS

Over the years I've tested about five hundred sex toys, and although there have been a couple of issues – like the time I answered the phone to a boss of mine on instinct, midway through testing a toy (I'm freelance; when the phone rings, you pick it up), or the time I had to review six sex toys at 6 a.m. in a Portakabin before a TV appearance – generally speaking, it's been a lot of fun. However, one toy that I was sent gave me more than I bargained for. It was orange. It was phallic. It was rubber. It was inflatable. And it was a strap-on.

I started off by trying it on to see how comfortable it was. So far, so good. I knew that it fitted snugly and suspected that it would be easy enough to use to do the job. Then came the testing of the dildo end. Unfortunately, just as I was about to try it out, the doorbell rang. It was a friend of mine, inviting me out for drink. I removed the strap-on and left it by the side of my bed to test out later.

When I returned, several hours and many cocktails later, it was still sitting there, and looked strangely inviting. I lubed it up, slipped it inside myself, then started inflating. Unfortunately, my drunkenness had dulled my sensitivity somewhat. It was only when it came to pulling the toy out that I realised I'd inflated it to its maximum girth, which was about the same size as my fist. Drunkenly trying to remove an inflated toy is not a good idea. I managed it, but the next morning I woke up with a desperate need to pee. It turned out that I'd managed to give myself what is popularly known as honeymoon cystitis with my overenthusiastic inflation the night before.

Since then, I've made a point of being sober whenever I test a toy – at least the first time. It's one thing ending up a little sore the morning after a night of passion, but it's just plain embarrassing when you get cystitis after a night of passion with yourself.

The very latest G-spot toys are designed for use with a partner rather than alone. One of them, the G-pilot, is shaped like an ice-cream scoop and designed to slip inside the woman, then angle the man's penis in the right direction. However, it's made from hard plastic, so unless you like the idea of feeling that pressing into your bits (when I tried it with my partner it took us all of thirty seconds before we had to take it out because it was hurting us both), it's not really worth the effort. Another option is the G-thrust, which looks like a pair of ankle cuffs (like handcuffs for ankles) with a piece of plastic between them that the woman uses to pull against the man's feet and angle him towards her G-spot. This is much more effective, although you may feel a bit of an idiot wearing the G-thrust as it doesn't exactly look sexy. Then again, having a good sense of humour will always make sex better, so it's certainly worth giving it a go.

Nipple stimulation

Once upon a time the only option for nipple stimulation, toy-wise, was nipple clamps. While these are all very well if you like firm nipple play, they can be a bit intense if that's not your bag. Luckily, the market has expanded and you can now get vibrating nipple cups that sit over your nipples and buzz away, leaving your partner with both hands free to use elsewhere, or suction cups comprising a squeezable bulb with a sucker that sits over the nipple and can emulate a partner sucking on your nipples. Either can be fun, although some of the suction cups can be slightly hard work to use, leaving you with tired fingers and thumbs. While nipple toys can enhance sex, there's still not anything out there, clamps aside, that's as good as the real thing, so they're better for solo play than for use with a partner.

Anal stimulation for her

Although for some women anal play is a top turn-on, many find the idea of it unpleasant. However, anal stimulation can indirectly stimulate the G-spot so, as such, it isn't something to be discounted offhand. If you don't try it, you won't know if you like it.

If you are planning on having anal sex, it's certainly worth investing in some toys, as you can get something that's smaller than a penis and use it to help accustom the anus to penetration. Taking a penis from a 'standing start' can be a little intimidating, after all.

When using anal toys remember the following:

- **Use a lot of lubricant.** This is the golden rule, as the anus doesn't self-lubricate and using a toy without lube is just asking for trouble, in the form of anal tears and fissures (small cuts).

- **Never insert anything into the anus that isn't designed for the purpose,** either by having a flared base or a string to pull it out. The anal muscles work differently from those in the vagina and it's all too easy for things to get stuck.

- **Start small and work your way up** (assuming, of course, that you want to; there's nothing wrong with starting small and staying small). And remember that vibrating toys feel larger once they're switched on, so take that into account when choosing one.

- **Never use anal toys in the vagina after use in the anus.** This can give you an infection and put you out of action: hardly the point of toy play.

In terms of options, there are butt plugs of every size, anal beads (including designer ones made of rose quartz) and anal 'stretchers' of varying sizes that are designed to help the anus get used to penetration over a period of time. It's definitely best to choose anal toys together unless it's something that you've discussed in detail, otherwise the receiving partner may feel put on the spot and pressured into doing something he or she doesn't want to.

Anal stimulation for him

One of the growth areas for sex toys in recent years has been anal toys for men. As society loosens up (ahem), men are beginning to realise that wanting anal stimulation doesn't make them gay (not that there's anything wrong with that) and that prostate stimulation can be damned good fun.

The prostate (also known as the male G-spot) is situated a few inches inside the anus on the upper wall. It feels like a walnut and swells when stimulated. By far the easiest way to find it is by slipping on a pair of latex gloves (having first cut your nails), lubing up your fingers then slipping a finger inside the anus, slowly enough that it relaxes around you. Never do this without warning. (Women's magazines have been responsible for a lot of men leaping out of bed in horror when their partner tried prostate stimulation on a whim, having read an article saying that men love it.) However, if you're both game for giving it a go, it can certainly enhance oral sex and will probably speed a man's orgasm to impressive levels.

Once you've dallied with anal play, you have various toy options: using a butt plug or anal beads, as with a woman, buying a specially designed prostate massager such as the Nexus or Aneros (both of which provide perineum stimulation too) or going the whole hog and getting a strap-on.

Strap-on sex for straight couples is becoming increasingly common. It's estimated that about a third of strap-ons are sold to couples for the woman to use on the man. Choosing a dildo or vibrator together is probably a good idea as many men are understandably intimidated about the idea of being 'taken'.

Getting the right harness is essential too, as otherwise the strap-on can move around making it tricky to position it so that it hits the prostate. You can get all-in-one harnesses that come complete with a dildo attached, harnesses that slip on like a pair of knickers and others that are worn around both legs with a central hole through which you slip the dildo. The latter two options allow you to use dildos of different sizes, making them best for beginners who want to start small and work their way up to something larger. Some harnesses include a hole to fit a vibrating bullet into so that the woman can get clitoral stimulation as her man gets prostate stimulation, which is an all-round winner.

As with anal stimulation for women, there are a few things to remember:

- Use a lot of lubricant.

- Go slowly.

- Start small.

Of course, masturbating your man as you penetrate him will give him a double-whammy of pleasure (assuming he's into prostate stimulation in the first place and not just trying it in the name of experimentation).

On a more flippant note, strap-on sex is also a great way to discourage an overly persistent male partner who is desperate to have anal sex on a regular basis, even though his partner's not that into it. Simply say, 'I will if you will', and you'll be amazed at how much more seriously your man will think about what he's asking for.

You big show-off

If you're both comfortable about the idea of toys, you may decide to put a toy show on for each other. You need only buy a porn video to see that, generally, men like the idea of watching a woman with a toy. However, while women in porn may get stuffed with the biggest monster plastic members around, it's far safer to opt for a toy that's either smaller than your man or non-phallic so that you don't intimidate him (unless you're getting into sub/Dom play, in which case a large toy may be exactly what you're after: to make the woman 'take' as much as is possible or humiliate the man because his dimensions don't match up).

And while male sex toys were once the thing of cheap jokes, you can now get masturbation sheaths that fit in the palm of the hand and don't look as risible as the classic inflatable doll, so putting on a masturbation show isn't just something that women can do for their partner.

Although you can put on a toy show simply to give your lover a visual treat, it's infinitely better if you masturbate as you really do when you're alone – that way, your partner will learn how you like a toy to be used on you, and be able to incorporate your favourite tricks when you use a toy together. However, you can always throw in a few moves that are purely there to turn your lover on. For women, slipping a finger into your own anus as you use a toy will probably give your man a thrill, as it suggests you're a 'bad girl'. Similarly, watching you penetrate yourself with a toy rather than simply using it on your clitoris will probably get his imagination going. Making eye contact as you masturbate with a toy will help your partner feel more connected to what you're doing, regardless of gender. And seeing a man ejaculate can be hot too, so if you're using a sheath, remove it at the point of climax to let your partner see the flow (or possibly feel it splashing over her body, if she's into ejaculate, which many women are).

Another fun and kinky way to use sex toys is to simulate group sex. If a woman has sexual fantasies about having sex with two men at the same time, her partner could emulate this by using a vibrator down below as he slides himself into her mouth, or vice versa. And if a man likes the idea of having a threesome, the woman can use a masturbation sheath on his member while she sits on his face. The Tenga is a new toy that's particularly effective for this kind of simulation: the vacuum makes it produce realistic squelching sounds and the interior is designed to feel as much like a real woman as possible, right down to having a simulated cervix; so all you need to do is close your eyes and you can immerse yourself fully in the fantasy.

Above all, let go of any feelings of self-consciousness when you put on a toy show for your partner. If you simply enjoy the stimulation and make sure that your partner knows they can take over at any point, you're bound to have a fun night.

Sex Furniture

If you search the Internet for sex toys, at some point or another you're likely to encounter sex furniture. While some of it can look intimidating to start with, it can actually be a great way to enhance 'vanilla' sex, rather than just forming part of a complicated sub/Dom scene.

By far the easiest type of sex furniture to incorporate into your sex life (unless you have limitless space or you don't object to turning your home into a sex den) is modular furniture. The two main brands are Loving Angles and Liberator, and both offer different-shaped foam wedges designed to help you get into positions that you might otherwise find awkward.

For example, there are triangular wedges that rest behind your head (make oral sex easier when you're lying on your back), or square cubes that rock back and forth if you turn them upside down (making doggie-style sex much easier on the knees because the man can sit down). And one of the advantages of this type of sex furniture is that unless someone already knows what it's for (in which case you've got nothing to feel embarrassed about, although you may not appreciate the knowing glint in your mother's eye), it looks just like ordinary modular furniture. Indeed, the shapes can be put together to form a sofa or armchair, which happens to be a lot easier to take up and down stairs when you move house, so it's got dual benefits.

Then there are sex swings. These come in two types: self-supporting and fixed. The former comes with a metal frame to which the swing attaches, while the latter has to be attached to the ceiling. (Screw your swing into the ceiling joist to avoid calamity, and don't consider it if you think your ceiling might not take the weight.) The swing itself is made from a series of harnesses that you sit on, and can be easily moved around to allow access to any part of your body. To use a sex swing, one partner sits inside it and the other one tilts them into whatever position they desire. Obviously, having the extra support means that you can get a lot more creative than you can without a sex swing, and they're ideal if you're into deep or G-spot stimulation. On the downside, however, you do need a reasonable amount of space to use a sex swing, so they're not ideal if you live in a small flat.

Although it's not technically furniture, it's also worth mentioning the Karma Sheetra – a sheet designed to help you experiment with different sexual positions. On it are numbered pink (for the woman) and blue (for the man) hand-, foot- and bottom prints, on which each partner positions their relevant body parts. Using the sheet gives you an opportunity to try out new positions without having to study a sex-position manual which, all too often, can read a little too much like a set of flat-pack furniture instructions: 'Insert part A into part B, while holding on to point C.'

If the idea of sex furniture is a little intimidating, don't be afraid to use your existing furniture to enhance your sex life. The humble washing machine has long been recommended as a makeshift vibrator, when on spin cycle – simply bend your lover over it, so that she can feel the vibrations running through her thighs and clit as you take her from behind. A sofa is great for doggie-style sex as the woman can brace against one arm while the man thrusts into her, making it easier for her to push back against him. And who can forget the infamous 'kitchen table' scene in *Last Tango in Paris*? Even if getting frisky with a pat of butter is taking things a little too far for you, if you look at your furniture with new sex positions in mind, you'll be surprised at how creative you can get.

Feet and Inches

Of course, when it comes to fetish, penetrative sex is only a part of the fun. One of the most popular body parts to attract fetishistic desires – particularly for men – is the foot. Although the sexual appeal of feet may be a mystery to anyone who doesn't find them a turn-on, foot fetishism is among the most common fetishes around. So let's put our best foot forward and find out more.

If feet are the object of your desire, there are foot-worship clubs, in which (largely) men can go to worship at women's feet, and thousands of websites offering the chance to buy used stockings, pantyhose, shoes and even toenail clippings. However, most foot fetishists don't require anything as extreme as someone else's toenails to get off. Instead, it's simply about appreciating a part of the body which is, in some ways, already sexualised. Shoes are often sold on the basis of their sex appeal – consider the term 'fuck-me boots', for example – and feet are also one of the few body parts (besides breasts and genitals) that are rarely seen uncovered, except when summer brings sandals into play, which makes them a taboo part of the body.

There are various ways in which to incorporate degrees of foot fetishism into your sex life. At the most basic level, you can simply give your lover a sensual foot rub. Start by bathing your partner's feet – something with a definite air of submission about it. Once their feet are clean, pat them dry, then kneel in front of your lover with one foot resting in your lap and wrap the other in a towel to keep it warm. Cover their foot in massage oil, then start by rubbing each toe in turn, using circular motions. Next, 'caterpillar' your fingers underneath their toes, circle your thumb over their sole, then their heel, and finish by softly rotating the ankle first clockwise, then anti-clockwise. Towel off any remaining oil, cover the foot that you've massaged with a towel to keep it warm, then repeat with the other foot. Even if neither of you has a foot fetish, giving a partner a foot rub is a great way to relax them, and relaxation is one of the keys to having great sex.

Should your partner have a foot fetish (and if they do, chances are they are male), you may want to indulge their fantasies a little further. Some men love the idea of painting their partner's toenails, and if the foot fetishism is part of a larger submissive fetish, you can always punish your man if he doesn't do it perfectly. Others want to lick or caress the feet, while some like the idea of being masturbated with a woman's feet. Then there are guys who like being trampled either by a woman in her bare feet or by a Mistress wearing high heels. Feet are surprisingly versatile, as illustrated by the numerous things that foot fetishists may demand of them.

TRUE CONFESSIONS
MY EX COULD ONLY GET OFF IF I RUBBED MY FEET IN HIS FACE

I wouldn't say that I'm a particularly kinky person but I did have a very odd experience with one ex. He admitted, drunk one night, that he was a foot fetishist, and unless my feet were involved he just didn't find sex a turn-on. I was surprised, to say the least, but it seemed like a harmless enough thing to try, so I asked him to explain it a bit more and I'd give it a go.

To say he was happy was an understatement. He told me that he wanted to start by worshipping my feet, so first of all he kissed and licked them, paying particular attention to my toes. I could hear him groaning (even though his mouth was full) and felt myself getting aroused, even though the sensation itself did nothing for me other than tickle a bit. Then he grabbed my ankles and pulled my feet hard into his face. I could see him rubbing his groin against the bed and guessed that he was pretty hard.

Once he'd licked my feet for what seemed like an age, he got some lubricant out of a drawer by the side of the bed and covered the soles of my feet with it. It felt really slimy and disgusting but I wanted to make his fantasy come true, so didn't complain. He asked me to 'assume the position', so I did, and he slid his penis in between my feet, gripping my ankles, and started to pull my feet up and down over his cock. It was quite pleasant feeling him getting harder for me, and his increasingly loud groans also really did it for me. I could see that he was nearing orgasm but I wanted him inside me so I asked him if we could have sex.

He wiped my feet down carefully and lovingly with baby wipes, then climbed on top of me, missionary style, and slid into me, raising my feet so that they were rubbing all over his face. Unlike previous sex sessions, he went wild. He licked and sucked my toes as he thrust inside me harder than I'd ever felt him before. I found it a bit distracting, but I loved the hard sex we were having and that soon blocked out the stuff he was doing to my feet. He stuck his tongue in between my big toe and the next toe along and immediately came inside me. I hadn't reached orgasm so he apologised and went down on me, facing my feet and still holding on to them as he did so.

Even though it was a sexier experience than I thought it might be, our relationship ended soon afterwards. Once he'd shared his fantasy with me he wanted to do it all the time. I told him that I wasn't the girl for him, as he clearly needed someone who shared his fetish; I wanted someone who found me sexy as I was, rather than needing my feet to be involved. The last thing I heard, he'd got together with a girl who was into the same things as him and I'm glad for him. It made him so happy, but I knew it just wasn't for me.

Angela, 27, nurse

Of course, foot fetishism isn't always just about the actual feet. It's also down to what the feet have on them. Different men like seeing their partner wearing different things. There's no one ideal but all the following have been listed by fetishists as appealing:

- ankle socks

- seamed stockings

- fishnets

- socks with pompoms on the heel

- platform shoes

- high heels

- thigh-high boots

- T-bar shoes

- ballet slippers

- ankle bracelets.

The only way to find out if your partner has a penchant of any kind is to ask. Don't be freaked out if they do confess to liking seeing your feet in a particular item. If your lover told you he adored seeing you in a halter-neck top, tight-fitting dress or stockings and suspenders, you probably wouldn't think it was odd in any way, so why should it be strange simply because they have a clothing preference that's a little further south? And, sometimes the fetish isn't as one-dimensional as it may at first seem. Certain items of clothing lend themselves to certain kinky behaviours which may be just as appealing as the garb.

TRUE CONFESSIONS

HE LOVES ME IN CHEAP TIGHTS – AND I LOVE IT TOO

My boyfriend Jeff has a thing about my legs. He's always telling me how beautiful they are and will often watch me while I shave my legs in the bath, then massage body lotion into my legs afterwards and kiss them all over. He particularly likes seeing me in short skirts, stockings and suspenders, hold-ups or fishnet tights. The fishnets are something that I've only grown to appreciate since I've met him.

I always thought that tights were incredibly unsexy. I've also always had a soft spot for rough sex – burglar fantasies, play fighting and all that kind of stuff. One night, I was getting ready for dinner at a nice restaurant with Jeff. I always like to wear sexy undies when we go out because chatting to him and flirting with him over dinner tends to get me in the mood. I realised too late that I didn't have any hold-ups or stockings without ladders in them, but I found a pair of fishnet tights tucked in the back of the drawer (a present from a friend for Christmas). I decided to give them a go because Jeff had mentioned he loved the way that fishnets look.

We had a great evening and got home feeling horny. We started making out on the sofa pretty much immediately and before long, things were heating up.

'I'm sorry, I've got tights on. I ran out of stockings,' I whispered as he started to push my skirt up.

'That's fine. I'll just have to rip them off,' came his instant response.

I must have let out a groan because he said, 'Oh, you like that, do you?' and flipped me over on the sofa. I wriggled around and pretended to struggle, but soon I was moaning as he slid a finger inside me. He started to call me a filthy girl, which always gets me going, and then I felt him rip my fishnets, pull my knickers aside and slide into me. He held me down and pulled my hair. I pushed back against him, wanting him as deep inside me as he could possibly go. He was relentless and only came after he'd made me come three times.

Now, I make a point of buying a pair of fishnet tights whenever I go to a discount store. I know that they're not going to last long whenever I put them on, and that's fine by me!

Alice, 36, lawyer

If the shoe fits

An obvious extension of foot fetishism relates to shoes and boots. While some people find them a turn-on because of the part of the body that they clothe, others are more into the way that they make (generally) a woman look. High heels are designed to make the buttocks stick out, the hips sway and the legs appear longer and tauter – all things that form part of the 'feminine ideal'. Indeed, Marilyn Monroe famously used to cut off a chunk of one of her heels to emphasise these effects.

High heels first hit the mainstream courtesy of a madam in the US who saw the effect that 'French heels' (named because a French queen had high heels specially designed to mask her diminutive height) had on men. In a keen business move, she equipped her 'best girl' with a pair, saw a massive increase in that woman's trade and promptly commissioned heels to be made for all of the girls who worked for her. As such, the link between sex and high heels has been there since they were first created.

Luckily, there are as many women out there with a passion for beautiful shoes as there are men that lust after women wearing them. By far the easiest way to indulge this fetish is to go shoe shopping together. While some men will find this incredibly dull, a shoe fetishist will find it unbelievably hot. Get your man to put the various different shoes on you then walk around wearing them, letting him admire your legs and see your body sway. And, of course, if a guy's a shoe fetishist you have the perfect excuse for being spoiled with lots of free pairs of shoes. And don't worry if you have a hard time walking in them. There's nothing to say that you have to wear them outside the bedroom at all. . .

'High-heeled shoes can be very dangerous to the ankles; some clever people have two sets – one for walking around in and one for waving in the air.'

Dossie Easton, sexpert and author of *Radical Ecstasy*

Shiny, Shiny Things

Of course, kinky clothing isn't just about what you wear on your feet. Look around almost any fetish club and you'll see that rubber, leather and PVC all tend to be pretty abundant. And it's hardly surprising that they're seen as sexy. All three are wipe-clean (making it easy to get fresh again after sex play), they cling to the body, emphasising its shape, and can also offer a degree of restriction that some people find sexy.

For some, the appeal of such fabrics lies in the fact that you're wearing a 'second skin', which is the closest thing to getting naked in public that you can legally get away with. For others, it's about the transformative attributes of such outfits: chances are, you'll look very different and, as such, will be able to assume a very different persona when wearing say, a rubber dress, PVC bustier or pair of leather trousers. You may find that your inner submissive or Dominant side creeps out if you wear kinky clothes. And then there's the taboo element: while fetish wear is creeping on to the catwalk, it's still pretty unlikely that you'll see someone walking down the high street in a rubber dress or leather kilt unless they're part of the fetish scene. High fashion aside, these outfits are designed for sex and, as with wearing sexy lingerie, that can be a turn-on in itself.

'Fetish clothing says, "I'm in the mood for sex", loud and clear. You haven't lived until you've worn latex clothing head to toe. Wash it in Woolite, don't wash it often and keep latex powdered if you want it to last.'
Annie Sprinkle, ex-prostitute and porn star and PhD sexologist

It's easy enough to incorporate rubber, leather or PVC into your sex life if you're curious about the way that it feels or looks. PVC is the most forgiving fabric as you can get a host of 'one-size' outfits. Plus, it tends to be lined, so it's relatively comfortable to wear. However, it can also be quite hot, so it's worth teaming it with something that isn't made of PVC: a cotton T-shirt with PVC trousers or a mesh vest with a PVC skirt. It's also reflective which means that it may not be flattering to the larger figure.

Leather is the second-easiest fabric to wear, but you do need to make sure that you air it thoroughly after every outing so that it doesn't smell, and get it cleaned relatively regularly by specialist leather cleaners. It's also worth looking after it properly by using a leather food to buff it up, as leather isn't the cheapest option when it comes to fetish wear.

At the hardest-core end of the spectrum comes rubber. Don't even think of trying to get into a rubber outfit without dusting the inside of it with baby powder first, otherwise you can end up with painful red marks on your skin. Also, make sure that you're thoroughly deodorised before you ease yourself in because there's no way that you can wear rubber without sweating. Once you're in, buff the outfit with silicone spray for the perfect finish. Or, better yet, get your lover to do this for you. It makes the rubber shine, which will only add to the appeal.

As these outfits tend not to be cheap, it's a good idea to go shopping together so that you can enjoy seeing each other in myriad outfits in the changing rooms without having to spend a fortune. You might even decide to make these shopping trips a regular occurrence and only actually invest in an outfit once you've had weeks of fun trying things on together.

Should you find that the smell of rubber, the shine of PVC

or the sensation of leather against your skin really gets you off, you can always take things further by investing in a sex toy made from your chosen substance. From butt plugs to spanking paddles, floggers to gloves, you'll be amazed at the wealth of products out there to explore.

TIPS FROM THE SCENE

I love fabulous fashion, but I think it's too easy to fall into the trap of believing that the only way you can look or feel sexy is to spend a fortune on your outfits, and then have to buy new ones to keep up with the times. Like any wardrobe decisions, look for items you can wear with various other trappings that offer multiple looks. Remember what you are going to do in these clothes: have you just bought a very expensive chastity belt? How will your beloved get at you in this outfit? Will those gorgeous steel spikes injure your lover in the heat of passion? I have fabulous outfits acquired in thrift stores or made from found objects from home.

Dossie Easton, sexpert and author of *Radical Ecstasy*

Highly Strung: the Appeal of the Corset

Another incredibly common clothing fetish is the corset. Designed to emphasise a woman's curves, this is hardly surprising. Men tend to be attracted to women with a 0.67 waist:hip ratio (the Golden Ratio) or hourglass figure, and a corset tends to shape women in such a way that they're closer to this physical ideal. And it's not just men that get off on seeing women wearing a corset. Some women enjoy the process of 'corset training' – teaching themselves to fit into ever smaller-waisted corsets – as they enjoy having a 'super-feminine' shape or the feeling of restriction that a corset can bring.

'When it comes to fetish fashion, start with a lace-up corset, whether you're male or female. To see your waist get inches smaller in front of your eyes is glorious.'

Annie Sprinkle, ex-prostitute and porn star and PhD sexologist

However, corset training shouldn't be taken lightly. You can cause major physical damage to yourself if you reduce your waist too much, unless you're used to the sensation and have spent time training your body to cope with it. Make sure that you see a professional corset fitter so that you know the way that a corset should fit and feel.

TRUE CONFESSIONS
MY CORSET MADE ME ILL

I've always liked the way that corsets emphasise the figure and had wanted to try one on for years. When I saw that there was a fetish fashion fair coming to a place near me, I decided that I'd go along to see what I could find.

When I arrived, I was a bit shocked. I hadn't been expecting there to be so many people wandering around scantily clad. However, I soon found a stall that took my breath away with its designer-made antique-style corsets that looked like something out of a period drama. There were endless different colours and styles: I settled on one that was the palest eau de nil, and trimmed with subtle gold embroidered birds.

I asked to try it on and was led behind a screen into a tiny back-room area. First of all, the lady asked me how big my waist was. I'd put on a bit of weight at the time, but didn't want to admit it, so I told her that I had a 24-inch (60cm) waist. She grabbed a corset with an 18-inch (45cm) waist, to give me an hourglass figure, she said, and put it on me. At first, it felt OK, but as she began pulling on the cords at the back to tighten it, I started to feel odd. I put it down to inexperience and when she dug her knee into my back to pull back hard and lace the corset tightly, I assumed that was the right way to do it. It seemed like she was pulling for hours, but when I finally turned around to look in the mirror, it was worth all the breathing in. My waist was tiny and my usually insignificant breasts were pushed up and out, looking as if they were bursting out of the corset.

Unfortunately, after a few more minutes posing in front of the mirror, I started to feel woozy. I asked her to unlace the corset. Even once she'd taken it off me it still felt as if I was being tightly gripped around my lungs by its bones. I leaned forward, feeling a migraine coming on, and had to take lots of deep breaths before I could finally stand up. I left the show shortly after that, feeling really peculiar, and when I got home I was violently sick, throwing up black stuff. I have no idea what it was but I genuinely thought I'd lost a body part.

Unsurprisingly, that put me off wearing corsets, until nearly ten years later when a friend managed to persuade me to give it a go. We were in a designer lingerie shop and there were some really pretty corsets, so, I picked out one that I liked the look of, although I still felt nervous, and took it to the woman at the counter.

'That won't fit you,' was the first thing she said. 'You need at least a couple of sizes bigger than that. You can only go four inches below your usual waist size.'

I was shocked, remembering the eight or so inches that I'd tried to reduce my waist by the first time I'd tried on a corset. No wonder I'd felt ill. She got the right size for me and led me to the changing room to help me into it. This time there was no fierce pulling, She explained that you're supposed to leave a gap of about two inches at the back of a corset when you lace it up rather than pull it all the way together.

When she'd finished doing me up, I stood in front of the mirror and admired myself. Although the effect wasn't as dramatic as it had been in the other corset, I still had the hourglass look. More to the point, I could actually breathe.

I came clean to the assistant about my earlier experience and she was horrified. I didn't buy the corset off her that day; even though I felt reassured, something about corsets still makes me nervous. But I'm going to a big party soon and am considering wearing a corset there. I love the way that they look and if it hadn't been for my first horrible experience, I'm sure they'd be a regular part of my wardrobe. I just wish I'd realised that you need to know about more than just fashion to help fit someone into a corset.

Claire, 28, journalist

For most people, wearing a corset is simply about emphasising the feminine form, pushing the breasts up invitingly and generally looking sexy. If you like the idea of wearing a corset but are intimidated at the idea of being laced tightly into a traditional boned number, you can opt for a soft-boned corset instead. These put less pressure on the ribs and are more comfortable to wear. You don't get the same degree of waist shrinkage as a properly boned corset can give, but you can always work your way up to that.

TIPS FROM THE SCENE

Buy a low-end corset in black satin or some other neutral colour/pattern. You can get one for less than £100, and wear it for non-fetish events like Christmas parties (so it's not wasted if you never go fetish clubbing again). It's guaranteed to triple your body confidence; *no one* looks bad in a corset! Wear it with some super-high heels, back-seamed stockings and either frilly knickers or a miniskirt and you're done.

Goldie, self-decribed submissive

Pony Play

Of course, you may find that kinky fabrics and corsets are just the tip of the iceberg for you, and that having dabbled in fetish fashion you want to go further.

Pony play is one of the more extreme fetishes that entails a degree of dressing up. Aficionados assume the role of either the pony or the driver, with the former wearing a corset-like harness, blinkers, reins and, in some cases, a horse-tail butt plug. The driver wears traditional riding gear, in many cases complete with whip.

Pony play is essentially a power game. The 'pony' is submissive, while the driver is dominant. Once in equine garb, the pony is allowed to converse only in animal terms: namely by responding to the tugs of the reins and the flick of the whip. While some people may see this as demeaning, that's really the point of the exercise – willingly handing over control to another person.

EMILY'S EXPERIENCES: *I PLAYED HORSEY WITH A STRANGER*

When I first heard about pony play, I was sceptical. I've never been particularly into horses and the idea of becoming one was just a little odd. Still, work is work, so I arrived at the fetish fair where I'd arranged to meet Sir Guy Masterleigh, the pony 'trainer', ready for whatever the day would throw at me.

Sir Guy was a charming gentleman, who instantly

put that me at ease. He told me that I could set the levels, and I didn't have to do anything I felt uncomfortable with. Although the idea of being trussed up and leading someone around in a corset was something I was prepared to do for a feature, I drew the line at having a horse's tail butt plug inserted, and he happily accepted my limits.

After stripping down to my underwear, I stood there while Sir Guy fitted me first in the basic harness, then added the blinkers and reins and finally attached me to the carriage that I was going to lead him around in. Although it looked heavy, the harness was balanced in such a way that it was perfectly comfortable to pull around, even once Sir Guy stepped into the carriage. What was less comfortable was the way that I had to behave: remaining silent – because ponies can't talk – and responding only to the tug of the reins or the flick of the whip rather than to any verbal commands. It was, as is exactly the intention, dehumanising, particularly as I had a bit between my teeth which, as well as preventing me from talking also made me drool, and the blinkers meant that I had extremely limited vision.

After I'd taken Sir Guy for a few circuits around the fetish fair, he untrussed me and told me that I'd been a good pony – something that felt strangely rewarding. However, I felt light-headed from the harness and shaky from the loss of 'normal' sensation I'd experienced: being unable to see properly or communicate verbally messed with my head.

I can understand why some people find pony play appealing as it's deeply submissive, but I'd rather keep my sex play more on the human side of the fence.

A variation of pony play is puppy play, in which the submissive partner is turned into a canine rather than a horse. A 'puppy' will eat out of a bowl, be led around on a dog lead and, in extreme cases, they may be forced to 'do their business' in the garden, rather than using the toilet. There's also the option to wear a puppy-tail butt plug.

Then there's kitten play, which, as the name suggests, involves assuming the role of a kitten. Similar to puppy play, it's slightly milder, involving wearing a collar and eating out of a bowl but omitting the punishment aspects that puppy play entails.

While assuming the role of an animal may be something that you find ridiculous, there can be something liberating about being freed from having to converse, instead responding to being stroked, tickled behind the ears and praised for being a 'good girl' (or, indeed, 'good boy'). You can dabble in this kind of role play with nothing more than a dog mask or a pair of pussy-cat ears, easily obtainable from any fancy-dress shop. If that makes you want to take things further, you can get most of the props you need from a pet shop (excluding the more specialist pony play kit), making it a relatively inexpensive way to try a new kink.

The Body Beautiful? Tattoos, Piercings and Body Modification

While most forms of fetish fashion can be put on and taken off according to your whim, some people prefer a more permanent way of amending their look. Tattoos, piercings and more extreme forms of modification, such as scarification (cutting patterns into the body and allowing scars to form), all have their place in contemporary society. For some people, it's a means of self-expression, while others take a more practical approach and use piercings to enhance their sexual pleasure: a tongue piercing to enhance oral sex, for example, or nipple piercings to increase sensitivity in the area.

TRUE CONFESSIONS
MY NIPPLE PIERCINGS MADE ME FEEL EXTRA SEXY

About twelve years ago I got my nipples pierced. At the time, I was with a bloke who'd had his done and I liked it lots on him. I got it pierced by an amazing man who used to be an army medic. He injected my tits with dental anaesthetic (he was allowed the drugs as he was a qualified doctor). It didn't hurt and it was a nice experience. When the drugs wore off though, it was really, really sore.

After the pain had settled down I just loved it. I worked in a night club at the time and all the security men loved the fact that I had my tits pierced. I was very happy to show them. To be honest I got off on the fact that they liked looking! I found it very sexy to think of boys thinking about my tits.

Over the years, for various reasons, I have taken the piercings out and put them back in again a few times. The last one I had was not such a great experience. It was done in a tattoo parlour by a moron. Generally, however, I've always loved having my tits pierced. It's like carrying an erotic secret, and has always made me feel very sexy. And it's not just having them on myself: I am bi and find woman with pierced tits sexy as anything.

After I had my piercing, I loved my tits being played with even more than before. I found it a huge turn-on and liked having the nipple rings pulled quite hard, but then I *am* pretty into pain of most kinds; biting and scratching both get me off so having an extra thing to tug at is great.

However, my husband was not massively into tit rings, so eventually they went. He was always worried about hurting me. I've tried explaining that I don't mind if he does but it's just not his thing and I don't want to force him to do anything that he doesn't want to do.

Lesley, 33, university lecturer

Tattoos and branding

Tattoos and branding (using a heated piece of metal to stamp letters, numbers or a pattern onto the body) can be used for purely decorative reasons or as a quirky way to express romance (say, by having a wedding ring tattooed on your finger or your lover's name on your bum). According to a poll from Harris Interactive, 42 per cent of women with tattoos say that it makes them feel more attractive, compared to 26 per cent of men, so it can affect your sexual self-confidence too.

However, tattoos also have a place in the sub/Dom world, with 'marking a slave' being one of the more extreme examples of power play. The 'marking' could be a word or phrase (such as 'slut', 'sissy' or 'property of . . . ') or a number, sometimes presented as a prison number in extreme fetish play. Alternately, a 'brand' with the Master or Mistress's initials may be used. However, permanent marking as a slave is a niche activity and much more common in sub-Dom erotica than in reality. If you like the idea of incorporating it into your sex play, by far the easiest way to experiment is with temporary tattoos. That way, you can enjoy the power kick of tattooing your partner without any risk of damaging them permanently or leaving them with a humiliating tattoo that seemed like a good idea in the heat of the moment.

Obviously, if you're looking at permanently modifying your body for real, you need to be prepared for a little pain. Choose a tattooist based on recommendation and take a painkiller an hour before you go to ease the pain. (Don't even think about getting drunk first – a reputable tattooist won't work on someone who's inebriated.) Generally speaking, the bonier an area is, the more it will hurt. However, you should also bear in mind the number of nerve endings in the area you're planning on having tattooed. The clitoris or glans are obviously going to be more sensitive than, say, the buttocks. And some tattooists will refuse to tattoo these areas, so you may need to shop around. (Then again, getting a genital tattoo really shouldn't be a spur-of-the-moment decision in any case!)

TRUE CONFESSIONS
MY BODY IS A WORK OF ART

I've had ten tattoos over the last five years and I'm aiming to get my whole body covered by the time I die. I love having my body turned into a work of art and put all my savings into having it done. It helps me attract the right kind of men too: I'm blonde with big boobs and used only to attract men who wanted a Barbie-doll type to hang on their arm like a trophy wife, which doesn't fit my personality at all.

Anna, 25, student

Once the tattooing process starts, your body will help to make it as painless as possible by releasing endorphins – natural painkillers – and some people find that they get a 'high' as a result of this (although, as with a sub/Dom-inspired endorphin high, they may need lots of affection on the 'comedown'). Once you've got through the process, it usually feels comfortable within twenty-four hours, and is virtually painless within a week.

Piercings

Having the nipples, tongue or genitals pierced can all enhance sex (*see* Case Study, below), both physically and emotionally, if you and your partner are into the idea. Having a part of the body pierced draws attention to it while, at the same time, marking you out as different from the 'norm'. As such, piercing is incredibly common in the fetish world as it gives kinksters a way to differentiate themselves from 'vanillas'. Of course, it also has a host of advantages when it comes to kinky play . . .

TRUE CONFESSIONS
HIS PIERCING GREW ON ME – BEFORE GROWING OUT

I wasn't initially sold on the idea of my then-boyfriend having a needle jabbed through his penis but after arduous Internet searching revealed that it could improve sex for him, it also (and as some would say, more importantly) suggested it could make sex more pleasurable for me. So how could I say no?

After deciding on the frenum piercing (through the stringy bit on the underside of the penis, also known as the frenulum), I sat in the studio waiting room while the deed was done and, upon hearing a stomach-churning shout of pain coming from behind the curtain, I was certain my sex life with that boyfriend was ruined for ever.

However, he soon emerged from the curtained room with tears in his eyes and a swagger John Wayne would have been proud of. I was relieved to hear that his manhood was still intact, but that penetrative sex would be off the cards for six weeks. I thought about all the foreplay and attention I would get while waiting for his poorly penis to get better and helped him hobble home with a smile on my face.

The coming weeks weren't really that exciting, though, because even the slightest stir in his pants had him doubled over in pain. So much for my sexually attentive boyfriend! The next two weeks frustratingly dragged so much that by early on in the third week my then-boyfriend assured me he was ready to try out his newly bejewelled crown.

The sex was amazing. Whether it was because it had been three weeks since I'd felt him inside of me, or whether it was the two-inch bar with large barbells on either side that made me wriggle with pleasure, I didn't care.

After the full healing time had passed, I have to say our sex life definitely improved. He seemed more sexually confident and I loved this new addition. Sure, new skills had to be learned; initially, oral sex felt strange as the barbells made it more difficult for me to deep-throat, but always one for the challenge, I revelled in the excuse of needing more practice.

After a month or so, we started to notice the bar was trying to push through the little bit of skin it rested under, but neither of us was that concerned because we both knew that a new piercing could often move about slightly before settling in one place under the surface. My then-boyfriend felt no pain, so we continued to have sex as normal until one day, I received a text message while at work, informing me that the piercing had eventually grown out and was now gone. And that was that. No pain for him, no bloody massacre, no tears.

With the piercing gone, the next time we had sex, did it feel different? Did either of us notice this lack of metal between us? No. So what actually had this piercing done to improve our sex life? Well, besides making us abstain from sex for longer than we would ever have liked, and given us something new and slightly taboo to look at and play with – nothing, really. It didn't make his penis bigger and it didn't give him longer erections; it just made our sexual experience slightly different, refreshed, if only for a while. So would I advocate male genital piercings? Well, they're fun while they last, but once the novelty wears off (or the piercing wears out!) I don't believe it makes that much difference. I would say save your man the pain and get a cock ring!

Lyla, 22, writer

If you decide that you want some sort of sexual piercing, there are a number of things to keep in mind:

- **Only go to a piercer who's been recommended.** (As with tattoos, ask friends who've tried the person you're considering or visit a fetish club and ask the most pierced person you can find where they'd recommend.)

- **Clean your piercing** using the solution provided. Although some people swear by it, avoid cleaning your piercing with tea tree oil as it'll keep the wound open which will mean it takes longer to heal.

- **Look after your health and take supplements** to boost your immune system.

- **Avoid touching your piercing until it's healed.** And you should not let anyone else (or their bodily fluids) anywhere near it either.

- **Don't use cosmetics or body lotion** on the pierced area.

- **Avoid going swimming** until the area has healed.

- **Go back to your piercer** if you see any sign of infection so that they can advise you as to what to do.

Some piercings heal in a matter of weeks while others take several months, depending on the extremity of the piercing in your, err, extremities. The clitoral hood takes only a fortnight to a month to recover, assuming there's no infection, while an ampallang or apadravya (*see* p. 176) can take up to eight months. Obviously, the fact that you have to avoid letting anyone's bodily fluids near the piercing until it's healed means that it can hamper sex. But good things do come to those who wait . . .

The hole truth: the many types of genital piercing

There are twenty main types of male genital piercing and eight female. Each has different benefits, healing times and end results, so check online for pictures so that you know what you're getting. Piercings do heal, but if you're letting someone near your genitals with a needle, it's better to be safe than sorry.

Male piercings

- **Prince Albert:** one of the more infamous genital piercings, this goes through the frenulum (the stringy bit on the underside of the penis head or glans) and urethra (the part a guy pees out of).

- **Reverse Prince Albert:** enters through the urethra and exits through a hole pierced in the top of the glans.

- **Ampallang:** runs horizontally through the glans and may or may not pass through the urethra. The latter is referred to as a transurethral piercing.

- **Shaft ampallang:** penetrates the shaft (main body) of the penis horizontally at any point along its length.

- **Apadravya:** penetrates vertically through the glans and is almost always placed centrally passing through the urethra. This is sometimes pierced in two sessions, the first to create a Prince Albert and the second (after healing) completing the apadravya. (This is thought to be the best piercing for pleasing a female partner as the top of it rubs against the G-spot during intercourse.)

- **Shaft apadravya:** through the shaft.

- **Hafada:** a surface piercing anywhere on the skin of the scrotum.

- **Transcrotal piercing:** passes through the entire scrotum from back to front or side to side.

- **Foreskin piercing:** surprisingly enough, a piercing that passes through the foreskin.

- **Deep-shaft piercing:** any piercing that passes through the penile shaft, most commonly placed behind the head of the penis.

- **Dolphin:** a Prince Albert that's attached to another deeper Prince Albert piercing, usually with a curved barbell.

- **Dydoe:** goes through the ridge of the glans.

- **King's Cross:** several dydoe piercings on one penis.

- **Frenulum ladder/Jacob's ladder:** a series of frenulum piercings extending from below the head of the penis to the base of the shaft.

- **Hafada ladder/guiche ladder:** as above, but with piercings extending to the anus.

- **Lorum ladder:** a series of genital piercings placed horizontally on the underside of the penis at its base, where the penis meets the scrotum.

- **Frenulum piercing:** on the underside of the shaft of the penis, almost always perpendicular to the shaft, and often through the frenulum. These are often designed to enhance sex for both the 'wearer' and his sexual partner. They can also be used to attach chastity devices to.

- **Guiche piercing:** through the perineum.

- **Pubic piercing:** at the bottom of the pubic mound, just above the shaft.

Female piercings
- **Christina piercing:** where the outer labia meet below the pubic mound.

- **Clitoris piercing:** through the clitoris itself. This is relatively rare and often confused with a clitoral hood piercing that pierces only the hood of the clitoris. It can be located vertically or horizontally, and is thought to enhance sexual pleasure (though the actual piercing process obviously hurts like hell as it's through the most sensitive part of the body).

- **Triangle piercing:** passes from side to side through the base of the clitoral hood (the small piece of skin that covers the clitoral tip) where it meets the labia, and under the clitoris. This is the only genital piercing that can stimulate the clitoris from behind.

- **Fourchette piercing:** a labial piercing at the rear rim of the vagina.

- **Isabella piercing:** a deep clitoral-shaft piercing from the clitoral hood to the top of the pubic mound.

- **Labial piercing:** through the labia, often done in symmetrical pairs.

- **Nefertiti piercing:** a vertical clitoral-hood piercing combined with a Christina.

- **Princess Albertina:** where the ring enters the urethra and exits through the top of the vagina. This carries an increased risk of getting cystitis, so is best avoided unless you really, really want it.

Of course, getting the piercing is just the beginning. Once you've had your nipples or genitals pierced, that's when the fun really starts. Having an area pierced can enhance sensitivity and change the way that sexual stimulation feels.

The pierced partner should test their pain threshold by incorporating playing with piercings into their masturbation sessions, then show the non-pierced partner what to do. You can also get small vibrators such as the Tongue Joy, which is attached to tongue piercings to add an extra buzz to oral sex. And there's no reason why you can't experiment with attaching these to other piercings too, as long as you clean it with alcohol after every use.

TRUE CONFESSIONS
I LOVE MY CLIT PIERCING BUT IT MAKES WORK INTERESTING!

I decided to get my clitoris hood pierced a few years ago because I love piercings. I felt that my boobs were too big to have my nipples done (I only think they look nice on small boobs), I'd had my hand pierced and it rejected, and as I was working in a prison at the time, I wasn't allowed any facial piercings. So all that was left was my doo da!

It was nowhere near as embarrassing as I thought it would be, mainly because the guy – yes, guy – was so cool. It was much less embarrassing and much less uncomfortable than a smear.

When I first got it done, every step felt like someone was having a rub! It was fabulous. I've never walked up and down the stairs so much in my life. I waited a week to have sex (it was the longest I could make myself wait) and it was great.

The constant state of arousal does wear off after a short time and then it really doesn't make that much difference to sex, although for DIY sex it does a bit. It's very tuggable, never sore and I still love it. My last partner didn't like it because it chipped her tooth but she's gone now and the piercing is back in. It hadn't closed up even after two years. My current partner loves it and plays with it often, as do I. She says that I use it like a comfort blanket. The only downside is that I've had some very funny experiences trying to get into high-security prisons (for work) when the metal-detecting wand passes my parts!

Andi, 28, prison warden

Don't even consider 'playing' until the area is fully healed, and, as with anything, start gently. While a piercing can stand up to a fair amount of pulling (I've seen a woman attach a pair of huge enamel jugs to her nipple piercings then spin around so that they fly through the air (admittedly as part of a 'grotesque burlesque' show rather than as a sexual kick, but it shows how much punishment they can take), it's safest to start by gently licking and sucking on the area and only moving on to soft tugging or harder suction as your partner gets used to the sensation. As with all sex, good communication is the key: as long as you go gently and ask your partner whether they're enjoying themselves every step of the way, you won't cause them any harm.

Sexual piercing and branding of your partner at home as part of a sex game aren't to be recommended either, unless you've been trained and are fully aware of all the health considerations. It's infinitely safer to use your imagination: blindfold the person who's to be 'branded' or 'pierced', then use the warmed back of a knife to press into your partner's skin while talking them through the (fake) branding or piercing that they're 'suffering'. Don't heat the knife enough to cause any damage – warm rather than boiling water is the key – but do spend a lot of time building the idea up so that your partner is fully in 'the zone' by the time you apply it. Alternatively, you can pinch your partner's nipples hard to simulate a nipple piercing or do the same to their genitals to simulate a genital piercing. Although the pain won't be as intense as a real branding or piercing, it's infinitely safer and with enough talking dirty, it can be surprisingly effective. You can also get clip-on nipple rings and genital jewellery to make the fantasy experience more convincing.

Are You Ready For More?

If you've tried everything in this book so far, you may well now have a fully stocked toy cupboard, a wardrobe full of sexy accessories and, possibly, a piercing that you certainly wouldn't want to show your mum. However, there's still more of the kink world to look at.

Power play is an ongoing theme in the fetish world, with bondage and sub/Dom helping you to explore your sexual roles and experiment with taking or acquiescing control in a sexual situation. But before we immerse ourselves fully into the world of whips and chains, rope and cat-o'-nine-tails, let's start with something altogether cheekier. Yes, it's time to assume the position and get ready for a good spanking.

CHAPTER FIVE

Spanking

The sound of a firm hand on a pair of quivering cheeks is something that echoes through hundreds of thousands of bedrooms every night. Yes, spanking is up there as one of the most common fetishes, with some surveys quoting figures as high as 80 per cent of women and 45 per cent of men finding it a turn-on. Unlike harder-core BDSM (*see* p. 215) practices, such as caning or whipping, it doesn't require any specialist equipment (unless you decide that you want to incorporate it), can be done with a relatively new partner without pushing either of your limits to uncomfortable levels and won't leave any serious marks. Yet it still has the potential to deliver a delicious high, courtesy of your body's natural responses. Is it any wonder that it's been recommended as a form of sex play in the most ancient of sex manuals, including the *Kama Sutra*?

Unlike some fetishes which have a purely psychological appeal, there are strong physical explanations for why spanking can deliver such a thrill. When you're spanked, your body responds – as it does to any form of pain – by releasing painkilling endorphins. And if a spanking is administered in the right way, you can encourage these endorphins to flood the body, causing a 'high' that some people compare to an out-of-body experience. Understanding how to create this high, as well as how to help your partner 'come down' afterwards in the most thoughtful possible way, will take your spanking experience to a whole new level.

While using the hand to spank is one of the easiest ways to indulge the fetish, you can get a host of spanking paddles and tawses (a paddle with a split down the middle) to increase the intensity of the experience. Some paddles are even embossed with words or phrases (such as 'slut' or 'bad boy'), so that you can temporarily 'brand' your partner with them, although this is best avoided if you're planning on wearing a skimpy swimming costume any time soon.

And then there's spanking aftercare. Making sure that you treat your partner in the right way once they've taken their 'punishment' will make a big difference to the quality of your experience. While you can simply give your partner a spanking then leave them to suffer, the whole spanking session will be so much more intense if you spend some time on afterplay too. Dusting the buttocks with baby powder or massaging a soothing lotion into your partner's reddened nates will help to make your experience more loving and intimate; and you can always start all over again once your lover has had a chance to recover . . .

TRUE CONFESSIONS
WHY I LOVE SPANKING

Spanking is the friendly end of BDSM. It's got a cheekiness and playfulness to it that getting out a heavy-duty reinforced leather cat-o'-nine-tails just doesn't. You can play with spanking and still believe you're vanilla. At the same time, you can't beat (ho ho) the flesh-on-flesh contact, which you don't get with expensive whips and paddles. There's nothing like feeling your partner's hand caress your buttocks after a few hard slaps have set your flesh burning. It simultaneously symbolises ownership and nurturing – everything domination and submission are about. The human hand is also a much more versatile and controllable weapon than a whip. You can go from light teasing to quite serious pain very easily. I once watched a friend's BDSM spanking video and, believe me, the girl's tears at the end were real. There's nothing 'wussy' about spanking taken to extremes. You can even leave hand-shaped bruises if you do it hard enough and the receiver's flesh is sensitive enough.

Goldie, 28, self-described submissive

Know the Risks

While spanking is one of the milder forms of pain play, there are a few rules that you need to bear in mind to avoid causing any lasting damage. Red cheeks are all well and good, but you don't want to prevent your partner from sitting down for a week. (Well, not unless they've been very, very bad.)

As with any form of pain play, communication – whether verbal or physical – is what BDSM play is about. You should take note of how your partner reacts and tailor your strokes to that. Establishing a safe word beforehand will mean that your lover can ask you to lighten up if things get too much for them. With spanking, the 'red, amber, green' code works particularly well, as it gives you the gradation required to take things up or down a notch, rather than simply halting proceedings altogether.

TIPS FROM THE SCENE

Alcohol and pervy sex play are a dangerous combination. Drink makes you clumsy and slack and, if you're spanking someone, you need to be careful to exercise appropriate restraint (no pun intended) and to know when your partner's reached their limit. Safe words are not enough on their own. The responsibility of brandishing that crop or that paddle involves recognising the point at which you need to stop; sometimes your partner might be so high on endorphins they don't even know it themselves. Being in charge involves knowing the boundaries and responding accordingly, while acting as if the boundaries do not exist.

Ian, 32, lecturer

You should remove any rings before spanking your partner to avoid accidentally cutting them. If your nails are particularly long, it's a good idea to file them down too. That way, you can get really into your spanking session without any risk of inadvertently cutting your lover (or breaking a nail). Alternatively, you can wear a pair of leather gloves to keep your nails out of harm's way.

Although the buttocks themselves can take a fair bit of punishment, striking the kidney area can be lethal, so you should avoid hitting the lower back at all to be on the safe side. Similarly, make sure that you strike fleshy parts of the body rather than any bones, particularly those in the back, to avoid causing damage. However, the buttocks and thighs will both take a good spanking, and focusing your attention on the sacral crease – the point at which the two meet – will mark you out as a spanking aficionado. Known as the 'sweet spot' it's thought to be the most sensual place to be spanked.

'Fresh bottoms wobbling and undulating to the thwack of my hand and the soft, yielding texture of a freshly spanked buttock is a wonder to behold – and hold.'

Mat Fraser, actor and compère of *Night of the Senses*

In order to give your partner the maximum endorphin rush, you should start spanking very gently and only very gradually build up to heavier strokes. That way, their body will have a chance to release some endorphins at the very start of the spanking, which will mean they can take more punishment (and enjoy themselves more) as you increase the intensity of your strokes. It also decreases the chances of leaving significant bruising (which can be a side effect of spanking if you go too hard, if your partner isn't used to it or if they have sensitive skin).

For the best spanking session, you should vary the type of stroke you use – there are so many different ways to do it that it's daft just sticking to one (added to which, you're more likely to get tired quickly if you keep slapping over and over again in the same way):

Use a wide, sweeping movement with the flat of the hand for loudly ringing slaps.

Use both hands at once (one on each buttock) for a more intensive 'no let-up' sensation.

Try rapid slaps on the thighs if you really want to inflict pain.

Aim at the tender insides of the buttocks, near the perineum, for that 'Where are they going to slap?' thrill.

Use just the tips of your fingers for more of a mild, yet stinging slap.

In addition, you can wet your hand to make the noise louder and the sting more intense, wear a leather glove to help prevent your hand from stinging too much as you administer the spanking and, of course, you can alternate each slap with a squeeze or stroke of the buttocks.

Don't forget the psychological side of things, either. Pulling your hand back hard for just a delicate tap of the buttocks will keep your partner on the edge, not knowing whether they should tense up or relax because they don't know how heavy the next stroke will be. And although spanking can be great fun all on its own, adding a little something extra to make your partner engage as fully as possible will only enhance the experience. So, as you slap your partner you could make them count the strokes, you can talk dirty to them or demand that they stay absolutely still, unless they want to earn more slaps. You can blindfold them then leave the room, only letting them know you've returned when they feel your hand across their buttocks.

It can also add to your lover's pleasure if you finger their vagina or anus in between spankings. Alternatively, you can use a vibrator on the clitoris or perineum as you spank to add even more of a pain/pleasure dimension to what you're doing.

TIPS FROM THE SCENE

Spanking causes a flow of blood to the area and its vibrations travel to the genitalia, resulting in a pleasurable tingling. It also releases adrenalin, endorphins and consequently feel-good dopamine. Build up strokes gently, achieve a steady rhythm, cup your hand rather than using the flat of your palm and alternate between teasing and tormenting. Remember, the sound is often worse than the sensation. Your hand, rather than their bottom, will probably smart more, although spanking need not be hard or painful to be effective.

Emma Gold, sexpert and author

But it's not just what you do to your partner that can make a difference. As the old song goes, 'It ain't what you do, it's the way that you do it', and varying the position can change the dynamic entirely. Being put over your lover's knee allows you to wriggle against them, while being bent over a bed with your hands tied is altogether more passive and submissive. If you're spanking a partner you might want to make them kneel on all fours while you tower above them, or you could decide to tie them, legs splayed, to a tree in the back garden. If you're strong enough, you could even drape your partner over your shoulder, fireman's lift-style, and take advantage of the fact that there's no way that they can escape. If you only try spanking in one position, it's the same as only having sex in one position: you'll only get to enjoy a fraction of the pleasures on offer.

Certain positions lend themselves to certain fantasies. If you like the idea of being a naughty schoolgirl, you might want to bend over a desk; and if you're more into the 'helpless prisoner' scenario, being spanked standing up with your wrists tied above your head could be more apt. If you find play-fighting a turn-on, getting pulled over your partner's knee and punished once you lose the fight could work best, while if it's a burglar fantasy that gets you off (or you're just into your comfort), being face down on the bed could fit the bill.

TIPS FROM THE SCENE

A comfortable bench/chair with a cushion on it to bend your partner over is always useful. It's really distracting if you have bits of furniture sticking in you or feeling the tops of your thighs go numb in the middle of a spanking. You can buy special spanking benches, but it isn't necessary. It might take a bit of time to find the right piece of furniture, but (luckily!) only practice will tell you when you've got the right one.

Goldie, 28, self-described submissive

Once you've chosen a position, and regardless of the fantasy (if any) that's going through your partner's head, one way you can build up to a really amazing climax is by administering your spanking in waves, each starting at a slightly higher level of intensity than the one before and going on for slightly longer. In between each wave, gently rub your partner's buttocks with the flat of your hand to soothe them, or apply a cooling or soothing lotion. (Make sure it's condom safe if you let it get anywhere near your lover's genitals and you're planning on having sex at any point.) Alternatively, try stroking them while wearing a fake fur massage mitt or glove for a truly sensual experience. For each new wave of spanks, start gently and slowly and then get into a good rhythm. Take it to the point where your partner starts yelping, then stop. As the endorphins start flowing, you'll find you can take it further each time.

When you really get going (assuming that this is what your partner wants), you can start taking it just past the stage where your partner thinks s/he wants you to stop, always giving just a few strokes more (but never beyond the point at which a partner has said the safe word – ever).

Some people like to beg you to stop, but want you to continue, and you should talk about this in advance, always stressing that the safe word should only be used when your partner really means no. If desired, you can take your partner right up to the point where they start crying, then take them in your arms and tell them how well they've done, or smother their buttocks in kisses. It's possible to make someone orgasm from spanking alone if this is done in the right way, and you'd be surprised how close it can make you feel to your partner.

Of course, spanking doesn't have to be limited to the buttocks. If you're feeling really cruel you can try spanking a woman's crotch or a man's perineum. However, if you do go for that option you need to start particularly gently, as it's obviously a lot more sensitive. If your partner has genital piercings, they should remove them first too, as you don't want them getting caught in the wrong way.

Once you've given your lover enough of a spanking, you have various options. You can rub soothing lotion into their cheeks. You can take a picture of their reddened buttocks and use it to threaten them when you're playing sex games in future. Or you could try something altogether more original.

'After spanking a feisty young filly, I dust her reddened buttocks with baby powder, then lick my finger and sign my name across them.'

**Man about town and professional cad,
Michael 'Atters' Attree**

When the spanking has fully finished, your lover will probably take a while to 'come down', particularly if it's been quite a long session, due to the endorphins racing around their body. Let them enjoy the sensation of elation, but gradually help bring them back into the present by massaging them, holding them and generally being affectionate. An endorphin comedown can be distressing and make your partner feel vulnerable, so don't assume your role ends when the spanking does. If your partner does get tearful after a spanking, hold them, reassure them that you love them and run them a warm bath. Hot, sweet tea is always a good option too. (Then again, I *am* British, so I would say that!)

Overall, spanking a lover with your hand is a safe thing to do, as long as they don't have any traumatic memories of being spanked as a child. Some people love it, others find it dull, some people giggle and some people come harder than they've ever come before. The only way to know the effect it will have on you is to give it a go.

TRUE CONFESSIONS
I BECAME A SPANKING CONVERT

I'd always found the idea of spanking a bit silly. Over the years, a few guys gave my arse a thwack during sex, but I soon put them straight, telling them that it just didn't do anything for me: spanking is something you're threatened with as a kid and the idea of it being sexual was totally alien to me.

That was until I met Simon. He was a perfect gentleman, but he also had an evil glint in his eye that drew me to him – every woman likes a bit of a bastard, after all. A few months into our relationship, our sex life was starting to tail off. It wasn't that the sex wasn't good, but it did feel like we were going through the motions a bit, and where I'd once have wanted to rip his clothes off the second he got home, now I was more likely to have a go at him for not wiping his feet when he came in and messing up my carpet.

One night, he came home after staying at the pub for an hour longer than he'd told me he would. He wasn't drunk, but I guess the beers he'd had made him feel a little less inhibited than usual. When I started to tell him off, he grabbed me, kissed me hard and said, 'Shut up, sexy.' I carried on, so he said, 'If you don't shut up, I'll have to make you.'

'I'd like to see you try,' was my instant reply.

The next thing I knew, he'd sat down on the sofa, put me over his knee and started spanking me. Unlike times I'd been spanked before, he started gently. I was cursing him, but he kept up a relentless pace and, after a little while, I started to feel a tingle downstairs, despite myself. I think I must have moaned because about two seconds later, he pushed my skirt up and pulled my knickers down, so that he could spank me bare-arsed. After a few slaps, he slipped a finger between my lips and discovered that I was wet.

'Well, you are a naughty girl, aren't you?' he said, and proceeded to punish me further for enjoying myself so much. He added a running commentary to his spanking: 'Oh, your cheeks are getting so red,' and, 'I can see you starting to drip down your thigh.' I was more turned on than I ever had been before and when he started to alternate spanking me with thrusting his fingers inside me, I started trembling. He kept me on the edge for at least an hour, until I was reduced to begging him for it. He still made me wait a little longer, but when we finally had sex, I came in seconds, feeling him pounding into me from behind, his thighs slapping against my poor, sore arse.

Now spanking is a regular part of our sex life and I often find myself deliberately playing up, just so that he'll punish me. And it makes me feel horny all day, when I can feel the remnant of pain as I sit at my desk at work, looking like butter wouldn't melt in my mouth.

Lucie, 25, designer

Going for a Paddle

Once you've thoroughly mastered spanking by hand, you may decide that you want to take things up a gear by incorporating some props into your sex play. You could use an everyday object such as a flat-backed hairbrush, a traditional wooden ruler, a plastic bottle (in which case the practice is called, originally enough, bottling) a table-tennis bat or a belt. Alternatively, you might choose to buy something specifically as a spanking aid.

The two main implements used for spanking are paddles and tawses. Both are available in numerous different styles, materials and sizes. At the milder end of the spectrum, you can get heart-shaped spanking paddles that have fake fur on one side and leather on the other, so that you can alternate sweet and tough love. At the more extreme end of the scale, you can get leather tawses with multiple tails that will be as painful as they are noisy to use.

You need to be even more careful with a paddle or tawse than you are with your hand. Never hit anywhere other than the buttocks and, as usual, start gently: you may not realise how hard you're hitting when you use a paddle because you don't get the stinging sensation that you do when administering a spanking with your hand. So don't go wild, and this goes doubly for rulers, belts and tawses as some may break the skin if used too violently. (If, however, this is part of the appeal of spanking for you, then never share your toys as it's a health risk.)

Again, you need to make sure that you deal with the endorphin comedown after a paddling. Keep your afterplay accessories (such as cooling lotions and soft fabric gloves) close to hand, so you can soothe your lover after you've punished them. After all, no one you love deserves to suffer all night. Do they?

Are You Ready For More?

So, now we've worked our way through fantasies and sexual displays, food sex, props and costumes. Plus, you know how to take your partner over one knee and give them what they deserve. But perhaps *your* answer to the question at the end of the last paragraph wasn't 'Of course not,' but instead, 'Bring it on.' Should that be the case, you may want to step a little further into the fetish world. If you like the idea of having a lover totally at your mercy – or, indeed, being captive to your partner's every whim – it may be time now to give a little bondage a go. After all, just because you're tied down with a partner it doesn't mean that you can't get tied up with them too.

CHAPTER SIX

Bondage

Most people experiment with a little bondage at some stage in their life, even if it's something as mild as being pinned down by a partner during sex. Scarves, ties and dressing-gown cords are regularly used for a purpose quite different from that for which they were intended, and you can buy novelty handcuffs in joke shops, gift shops and, obviously, the numerous high-street sex shops that are now found in almost every town.

Given that sex is, at least in part, about giving yourself to a partner, the urge to take that one step further and put yourself entirely in a lover's hands can be compelling. By allowing them to tie you up, you're showing that you trust them completely. As such, it's certainly not something to enter into with a partner who you don't trust because when it comes to bondage you need to feel secure (ahem) and be very aware of safety guidelines. Serious physical (and possibly psychological) damage can be inflicted by getting it wrong.

Luckily, there are numerous ways in which you can enter into bondage in a mild way, so you can test the waters before diving in at the deep end. You can buy handcuffs made from feathers that offer more of a psychological than a physical restraint, as they're fragile enough to break out of in seconds.

You can tie someone up by wrapping their hair around their wrists which, if you're into a bit of pain play, has the added bonus of making it harder for them to struggle, as it'll pull their hair, but again, it is very easy for them to get out of. Clingfilm (aka Saran Wrap) can be used to wrap around your lover's wrists, and if you use a single layer, it's easy enough to snap. You can get kitsch and use liquorice bootlaces to bind your lover's wrists, go for a cheap DIY approach and use toilet paper or simply keep your partner in mental bondage by ordering them to lie entirely still and not move a muscle while you pleasure them.

Once you feel comfortable with bondage, there are, of course, numerous stronger types of binding that you can use to take things further. From Spankties to handcuffs, wrist and ankle restraints to spreader bars (for more on all of these, *see* pp. 207–209), you can truss your lover up in so many ways that there's no need for it to ever get dull. And if you fancy getting artistic, you can always incorporate some Japanese rope bondage (*see* p. 210) into the proceedings and turn your lover into a work of art. But before you get into any of that, you need to (ahem) know the ropes. By knowing all the safety guidelines, you can make sure that you don't get yourself tied up in knots.

TIPS FROM THE SCENE

Bondage requires a lot of technical information – there are tons of ways to do it wrong. When you are learning, be ready to hear that somebody's tendons hurt and undo whatever you've done and do it again. This will happen a lot until you get the hang of it. Bodies are complicated, and not originally designed to be tied up.

Dossie Easton, sexpert and author of *Radical Ecstasy*

Know the Risks

Although you can dabble at the very mildest end of bondage play without any risk, using feather cuffs or liquorice bootlaces as described above, it's worth understanding the basic guidelines anyway; that way you can up the ante as you both see fit in the heat of the moment, without coming to any harm.

To start with, while it may seem like common sense, and should go without saying: never restrain someone against their will. Not only does it break the safe, sane and consensual rule, making it an unethical (and illegal) thing to try, if someone is struggling, it's all too easy to tie them up in a way that could hamper their circulation leading to pins and needles, general discomfort and nerve damage.

Even if you play consensually, there's still a danger that you might tie your partner too tightly and cause damage to their nerves. To avoid this, when someone is restrained by their wrists or ankles make sure that you check their extremities (hands and feet) regularly to ensure that they're not going cold (which is a sign that you've blocked their circulation). If the extremities do feel cold, you should untie your partner immediately and massage their hands or feet to help restore blood flow.

Never, ever, *ever* tie anything around your lover's neck, as this can cause asphyxiation. While some people do practise erotic asphyxiation, it's *extremely* dangerous and can cause brain damage or even death. The cause of death isn't generally strangulation, but instead tends to be a heart attack induced by lack of oxygen in the bloodstream. Other risks include rupture of the windpipe, fracture of the larynx, damage to the cervical spine and dislodging fatty plaques in the neck artery which can travel to the brain and cause a stroke. Even tying or gripping your partner's neck tightly for as little as ten seconds can cause brain damage, so this is not a rule to be trifled with.

Then there's the issue of what to use. When it comes to restraining your partner, bondage tape is safer than rope as it doesn't tighten if your lover struggles. Rather than traditional sticky tape, bondage tape sticks to itself but not to skin, meaning that there's no pain when you remove it. It's inexpensive and can also be used to create makeshift fetish outfits should you get a last-minute invitation to a kinky party that you simply can't refuse.

If you decide to go with the rope option, you should always make sure that you tie your knots loosely enough so that you can untie them at speed. There are numerous knots that you can use, ranging from the simple to the complex, with online video tutorials that explain how to tie them all (just search for 'bondage knots' on the Internet). However, the one knot that should always be avoided is the slip knot as this can tighten during sex play. If you don't want to look at the online tutorials,

TIPS FROM THE SCENE

If you're tying someone up, however loosely, you need to be sure you can untie them at a moment's notice if they suddenly get pins and needles or need to go to the loo! You don't want to be fumbling around, trying to work loose a tightened knot when your partner wants to escape. Make sure you put any keys in a safe, high place, where they're not going to get knocked onto the floor or down the side of the mattress. Candles can be sexy, but be sure they're well out of the way. The last thing you want is to have to fireman lift your still bound-and-gagged partner out of a burning building after knocking over a bowl of floating candles with the tip of your bull whip.

Ben, 27, artist

just use a simple bow (much as you'd use to tie your shoelaces), as this can be undone rapidly. You should also make sure that you keep a pair of scissors to hand, so that you can release your partner quickly if the need arises. Similarly, if you're using handcuffs, keep two sets of handcuff keys nearby (it's always best to have a spare just in case you lose the first set) and if you're going for seriously kinky play with metal spreader bars, keep those bolt-cutters handy.

Once your partner is restrained, don't leave them alone – not even for a minute. If you're playing a power-play game, you can always blindfold your lover and pretend that you've left the room. And although it's often more tempting to play sex games when you're feeling a bit tipsy, it's best not to try bondage when you're under the influence of drink or drugs, as you might misjudge how tightly to tie the knots or, as the restrained person, be unable to establish your comfort levels in an accurate way. There's also the risk that the restrained person might vomit when they're unable to move their head which could lead to choking – never a good way to enhance the romance in an

---

TIPS FROM THE SCENE

You've got to be really careful what you tie someone up with and where you tie them. I had a partner who thought it was fine just to grab some very old and hard piece of rope, knot it around my wrists and then leave me hanging from the bedhead with the weight of my top half on the knots. It was not. My wrists went numb very quickly (I had a friend who caused permanent nerve damage to his girlfriend's wrists by doing that and she never got feeling back) and it was extremely uncomfortable and rather scary. When something like that happens, you can't concentrate on enjoying what's going on and it just renders the whole thing pointless. If you're going to try Japanese rope bondage I'd suggest doing a class held by a scene expert (try londonfetishscene.com for ads) and buying some proper soft rope intended for the practice (try Quality Control online). Otherwise, I wouldn't recommend using rope at all. Buy some proper bondage cuffs that you can attach to a bedhead. Spreader bars are great too. For 'soft' bondage, you could just use ribbons.

Goldie, 28, self-described submissive

evening. And if you're really hammered, you might pass out which can be equally dangerous whether you're the one who's tied up or doing the binding.

If you get really into tying each other up and decide to dabble in Japanese rope bondage (*see* p. 210), never suspend anyone unless you're trained in suspension bondage, and even then, be extremely careful. If someone is suspended, their full body weight will be pressing against the ropes if you don't know exactly what you're doing, and this can obviously be extremely hazardous, if not lethal.

It may sound like a lot to consider, but the rules will come naturally once you've played a few times; and when it's your lover's safety at stake, it's well worth taking a little time to ensure that you know what you're doing.

That said, if you're just enjoying mild recreational bondage, it's really nothing to be concerned about. Having a partner tied up to receive pleasure (or pain, although sadomasochism and bondage are by no means twinned) can give you a huge power kick and some people find that it's only when they're restrained that they can fully give in to their sexual desires. After all, they can't do anything about the situation they're in (or so the mental dialogue goes), so they may as well just relax and enjoy it.

TALES FROM THE SCENE: I LEARNED TO LOVE BONDAGE AFTER FIFTEEN YEARS AS AN ESCORT

I worked as an escort for about fifteen years before I ever understood the appeal of bondage. During all those years of working as a sex professional, I had beaten, spanked, blindfolded, tied up and handcuffed more men than I can remember. And yet my experiences didn't match the personal anecdotes I had listened to from both lifestyle and professional practitioners of BDSM.

After I retired from escorting, I became curious about being on the other side of the whip and the rope. So, during a lecture tour to Seattle last year, I was tied up and spanked by the beautiful Mistress Matisse. I was shocked by how absolutely free I felt once I was blindfolded and bound by rope. Although I was bound so tightly I could barely breathe, I felt more emotional freedom than I had ever experienced in my life. What an irony. In that moment, I finally knew that one is never so free as when they have surrendered all control.

Veronica Monet, certified sexologist and author of
Veronica Monet's Sex Secrets of Escorts:
Tips from a Pro **(Alpha Books, 2005)**

Tie Me Up, Tie Me Down

Once you understand all of the safety guidelines, it's time to get into the sexy bit: actually tying your lover up. A whole host of options is available to you, ranging from the mild to the extreme.

Starting Out

At the tamest end of the scene, you can use something that is weak enough for your lover to break out of if they feel uncomfortable (although as long as you have your safe word in place, that shouldn't be an issue, as you can simply remove any restraints the second your partner asks you to). In addition to the ideas outlined on p. 198, you could use a bundle of long grass if you're opting for outdoor action against a tree, a cheap chain necklace with a link or two loosened so your partner can snap it by pulling their wrists apart or a length of marabou feathers for glamorous appeal.

If you're looking for something a little stronger, but are merely curious about bondage and would rather not spend any money, try something that you already have in the house. As already mentioned, ties, scarves and dressing-gown cords can all be used to restrain a partner (though never use anything that you really value – there's always the chance that you'll have to cut your partner out of their bonds if the knots get too tight and you won't want to destroy your favourite tie in doing so). Although tights and stockings would seem fit for the purpose, they are less than ideal as the knots can tighten to ridiculous levels and the fabric can dig in uncomfortably (as I discovered in an early bondage experiment, *see* below). As such, they're best avoided.

EMILY'S EXPERIENCES: MY MASTERCLASS LEFT ME TIED UP IN KNOTS

Like most people, I've experimented with bondage with partners over the years. I remember one experience in my late teens, when I was still living with my mum. My long-term boyfriend and I decided to try bondage using tights to tie me down. After we'd finished, the tights were so tightly knotted around the bed that I couldn't remove them. I went downstairs to get some scissors, but before I'd had a chance to remove the tights my mum went into my room and asked me why there was a pair of tights tied to each corner of my bed. All I could think to say was: 'I was trying to stretch them.' I don't think she was convinced.

Fast forward a few years (well, about fifteen) and I was sent to a bondage masterclass for work. The lovely Mistress Absolute took us through all of the safety guidelines, then taught us how to make a basic body harness out of cotton rope. I was amazed at how simple it was and impressed by how beautiful the end result looked.

Mistress Absolute explained that we could use what we'd learned to tie our partners up in numerous ways, and called me out of the audience to demonstrate. And so it was that I found myself lying face down on the floor, fully clothed, with my ankles and wrists attached to each other in a classic hog tie. The only part of my body that I could move was my head, and even then my movement was severely limited. Although it was a little too confining for me, I admired her mastery (or should I say Mistressry?), and have subsequently used what I was taught to hog-tie a partner who was considerably bigger than me. That's one of the joys of bondage done properly – you can restrain someone who's easily capable of overpowering you when rope isn't involved, and then treat them as you will . . .

Spankties and silk or cotton rope

Moving slightly higher up the bondage chart, you can now get a great product called Spankties. These resemble the foam-covered wire hair curlers that were big in the 1980s, but are considerably longer, so that you can wrap them around your partner's ankles or wrists. Unlike handcuffs, you simply twist them to keep them in place, making them easy to remove and alleviating any concerns about losing the key. As an added bonus, you can also twist them then use them to spank your partner (hence the name).

If you want to take things a little more seriously, try silk or cotton rope (both of which are cheaper to buy from a magic shop than a sex shop, if you have one in your area). They are less likely to knot too tightly to be undone at the end of your bondage session, and they look much sexier (and less ridiculous) than a dressing-gown cord.

Handcuffs

Next come handcuffs. These are available in numerous different types, ranging from lightweight feathers to 'fun fur'-covered plastic, 'one-key-fits-all' metal cuffs to police-issue heavy-duty cuffs that would take an escapologist to get out of. Generally speaking, the more secure the cuffs, the higher the price. You also pay extra for things like velvet lining (to prevent wrist chafing when you struggle) and designer trim, such as diamanté, for those who fancy a little bit of burlesque glitz when they're indulging in bondage games.

Wrist and ankle restraints

Similar to handcuffs, these are usually more comfortable to wear and less likely to leave marks. Comprising thick bands of fabric (from velvet to leather, PVC to fake fur) with a fabric link between them, handcuff style, they are ideal if you like the idea of tying your partner down spreadeagled, as handcuffs on the ankles can dig in uncomfortably and chafe.

Spreader bars

At the most extreme end of the spectrum are spreader bars. These consist of cuffs attached to a length of metal, wood or some other material, that keep your partner's arms or legs splayed at a certain distance. Though you can make your own using rope, it's quite a complex process (but again, there are online video tutorials available), so it's infinitely easier to buy them. Some spreader bars are adjustable, meaning that you can increase the distance to which you spread your partner's arms or legs during your sex play, should you so wish, while others are static. Your best bet is to go to a fetish shop and try on some different spreader bars. The shop assistants have seen it all before, and will be able to make recommendations as to which is best for you.

TIPS FROM THE SCENE

Don't spend huge amounts of money on pervy bondage gear. Invest in some good-quality wrist and ankle cuffs, maybe a collar. Hardware shops are an invaluable source of BDSM accessories: snap locks, clothes pegs, ropes, chains, padlocks – all you need to tie someone to the bed, a chair or themselves. A length of tube with a rope running through and two snap locks either end makes an inexpensive leg separator. A clothes line cut into pieces will provide you with all the restraints you need. Pallet wrap is great for mummification. Use your imagination and you can have your own DIY dungeon.

Lizzie, 35, fetish model

(**Note**: before making your own kinky gear, do check that it's safe with someone who is familiar with the scene. It's best to err on the side of caution.)

Regardless of the way in which you restrain your partner, there are numerous things that you can do once they're powerless. You can give them repeated orgasms knowing that they're unable to stop you. You could apply ice to their most sensitive areas (but remember to suck it first to melt it slightly, so that you don't give them ice burns), then follow it up with warm kisses. You can spank, whip or paddle them, or put on a masturbation show, in the knowledge that they can't touch you and will probably be feeling more frustrated by the second.

Discuss the various options with your partner in advance, so that you know what they like the idea of and what will leave them cold, and won't have to break the 'scene' once they're restrained. After all, just because your partner is the one who's tied up, it doesn't mean that they are any less than equal in the sex games that you're playing.

> *'I love the feelings of helplessness, the power exchange; I particularly like the slight dehumanisation of losing the use of my hands. Standing bondage actually provides support so you can stand up for longer and get more done to you. And tied to the bed, you can pull and yank and thrash all you want without knocking your lover to the floor.'*
>
> **Dossie Easton, sexpert and author of *Radical Ecstasy***

Japanese Rope Bondage

Should you discover that bondage is something that you and your partner both find arousing, you may decide to take things further by experimenting with Japanese rope bondage (or to give it the correct name, *Shibari*). This is an extremely specialist type of rope play which is as much about beauty as kinkiness. Elegantly positioned knots and exquisitely tied bonds are used to bind your partner in intricate ways. Japanese rope bondage can also be used to suspend people, although this is something that should only be done if you've been trained by an expert. As such, you should never try to emulate any Japanese bondage that you may see online involving suspension (or, worse, make up a knotting system of your own).

TIPS FROM THE SCENE

Do not imagine you can copy all the gorgeous bondage you see on the Internet. I have all too often looked closely at a lovely scenario wondering, 'How did they do that?' only to discover that they did it in Photoshop.
Dossie Easton, sexpert and author of *Radical Ecstasy*

At the simplest end of the Japanese rope bondage spectrum is the body harness. Do not use this to suspend anyone, follow all the safety guidelines and be particularly careful about ensuring that there's nothing tight around the neck and that you use the right type of knots. Slip knots should be avoided at all costs.

Almost anyone can make a harness which looks impressive, yet is incredibly easy to do. First of all, you need about 20 feet (6 metres) of rope. Silk rope will chafe less than cotton, and don't even think of using hemp rope, unless you really want to hurt your partner.

1. Start by folding the rope in half.

2. Form a loop that's big enough for your partner to put their head through, and slip it over their head, leaving the knot resting on their breastbone.

3. Get your partner to stand up, and using the two lengths of rope that you now have dangling down, tie another knot in the rope at their solar plexus, another at their navel, and another at their clit or perineum, depending on their gender.

4. Now bring both lengths of rope between their legs and up their back to feed through the loop behind their neck.

5. Standing behind your partner, let the rope drop down their back.

6. Separate the two ends and wrap them around your partner's torso, hooking them underneath the knot at their breastbone.

7. Pull the cord back to loop between the two lengths of rope running down their back.

8. Separate the strands again and loop under the knot at the solar plexus.

9. Pull the rope back once more to loop through the two strands of rope running down their back.

10. Pass the rope forward again to loop under the knot at their navel.

11. Finally pull it back again to pass through the back rope once more then tie it in a neat bow.

(It's way easier than it sounds and can be done in under five minutes once you've had a bit of practice!)

You now have an impressive-looking harness and, if you pull on any of the knots, you'll find that their positioning allows you to move someone who's significantly heavier than you are around. You can add to this harness by tying another rope through the back of the neck loop to use as a lead (never, *ever* tie a rope directly around someone's neck as you could inadvertently strangle them) or by making your partner lie down (by pulling them to the floor using the knot at their solar plexus), then tying rope around their ankles and looping it through the back of the neck loop to render them utterly helpless. What you do then, of course, is entirely up to you.

TALES FROM THE SCENE: *WHY I LOVE BONDAGE*

Japanese-style rope bondage is very beautiful to look at – some people see it as an art form as much as sex game. It can also be done so that the knots rub on particularly sensitive parts of the body and you can bring about orgasm just by tugging at the right bits. For me, though, the attraction of bondage is the sense of total helplessness. Because all choice about movement is taken away, it's possible to totally lose yourself in your physical sensations. I also like the idea of being an object during sex rather than a person, so anything that makes me unable to react like a person (i.e. to move, respond, escape) helps with that.

Goldie, 28, self-described submissive

Are You Ready For More?

You've now learned how to restrain your partner in all manner of intricate and exciting ways. However, this could well be just the beginning, opening your mind to a whole host of other kinks. Tying your partner up or being bound by your lover may well bring your submissive or dominant feelings to the fore. You might even decide that you want to take things further and throw some punishment into the mix. That doesn't necessarily mean inflicting pain on your partner, although whips, crops and clamps do certainly have their own charms. It may involve humiliating a partner, 'training' them to come on command, treating them as your sex slave or experimenting with kinks like watersports together.

Yes, you're about to enter the world of submission and domination. If you get scared, the safe word is 'aubergine' . . .

CHAPTER SEVEN

Submission, Domination and Beyond

It's hardly surprising that bondage and spanking are often lumped together with submission and domination under the uber-efficient acronym BDSM (which stands for bondage and discipline, dominance and submission, and sadism and masochism – six types of fun in four little letters). While the endorphin rush of a spanking and the acquiescence of being bound can both be enjoyable in their own right, there's a strong chance that you might find some of your darker cravings coming to the fore once you open the Pandora's box that is kinky play.

While some people claim that BDSM is about one partner controlling another, and that, as such, it is abusive, that's completely untrue. Although there is obviously a power exchange going on when you're indulging in sub/Dom play, it should be entirely consensual with both parties getting equal pleasure from it. You might well get a thrill out of being the passive partner in a sexual encounter, get off on the idea that you're being punished for your 'sins' or simply enjoy having pain inflicted on you in a loving way.

However, if you don't like the thought of being submissive, don't submit. Equally, if you are filled with dread at the idea of being dominant (a Dom if you're male, Domme if you're female, jointly described as Dom/me), you should not feel remotely pressured into ordering your partner around. (Aside from anything else this would put you in an oxymoronic sexual situation.) The only way that sub/Dom play should enter into a relationship is if both partners are equally curious about the pleasures it can bring.

'When we put ourselves in the hands of another, we not only lose control, we lose ourselves, providing brief respite from the otherwise constant maintenance of our ego. Physical pain distracts us from our emotional pain; our worries and fears are forgotten. Nothing else exists except our body. Finally, we're out of our minds. Post-pain sex is far more intense.'

Emma Gold, sexpert and author

If the idea of pain is an instant turn-off, but you like the idea of experimenting with different sexual roles, don't panic. It's entirely possible to indulge a sub/Dom fetish using nothing other than your mind. In fact, power play is just as much about the mind as the body, if not more so, and giving someone a sexual high through words or looks alone can be an intense experience, as can orgasm control, in which you 'train' your partner to climax on command.

But obviously, sub/Dom does take a physical form too, through anything from spanking and hair pulling to caning and whipping. As long as any pain that's administered is safe and by mutual consent, rather than out of anger or spite, then it's just adding an extra layer to your sex play. And while the law (nosily) generally tends to have issues with people inflicting lasting damage on a partner, even with consent (do an Internet search for the Spanner Trust for a full explanation of some of these), if you stick to a bit of slapping, clamping and general play with whips and crops, you'll be fine. (As long as you don't post pictures of what you've done on the Internet, that is, due to absurd US and UK censorship laws, but that's another issue entirely.)

Exploring the different sexual roles that you can assume could well revitalise your sex life. It's amazing how easy it is to fall into a rut when you're in a long-term relationship. Playing the Dom/me, however, can open up the way for you to make sexual demands that the 'normal' you would be too scared to make. And conversely, submitting to your partner may make you feel more willing to indulge in sex acts that you'd usually decline. As such, sub/Dom play has a wonderful way of making your boundaries a little more elastic, and helping you to push your limits further than you may have wanted them to go before (but never without your say-so).

And sub/Dom doesn't have to be a one-way street either: you can always 'switch' (the kinkster term for taking it in turns to be the dominant or submissive partner). That way, not only will you be able to get your own back if your Dom/me is particularly cruel, but you'll also discover the joys that both sides of the sexual coin can bring.

TALES FROM THE SCENE: WHAT SUB/DOM MEANS TO ME

I like to say 'top' and 'bottom' rather than 'Dom' and 'sub' when I talk about BDSM. This is because to a lot of people on the fetish scene, Dom and sub are loaded terms that say something fundamental about a person's nature, while the terms top and bottom just describe particular roles that can be played within BDSM scenes and don't make any statements at all about the people who are playing them.

I think everyone inclines towards one or the other (and some people are lucky enough to swing both ways). Some people claim that tops are ego-based personalities (who get the biggest buzz out of perceiving themselves to be in control of others) and that bottoms are id-based (they get the biggest buzz out of losing control and feeling their personalities dissolve), and I think there's something in that. However it works, though, I think the main appeal for couples is the incredible sense of trust, understanding and connection it can help you build up.

For a top, knowing that someone trusts you enough to let you hurt them/tie them up/order them around is a huge buzz. For a bottom, being able to let go of control and knowing that your partner will take care of you and is focused totally on you is a buzz. Playing in these roles is like going on a journey, just the two of you, and knowing it's only going to work if you stick together. You have to be highly aware of each other's reactions the whole time. When you come out the other side of that journey, you feel incredibly close. And the orgasms really are mind-blowing.

I once had a partner tie me up and flog me for about two hours. In between beatings he stroked and then penetrated me with his fingers so that I got gradually more and more turned on. Eventually, I lost all sense of who or where I was; I was totally focused on him and the sensations that he was giving me. When I came, it was like my entire body expanded and contracted, from the tips of my toes to the top of my head. I felt like I was floating. It took me hours to get back to normal! Afterwards, he was immensely proud of himself and I was extremely grateful to him. We had never felt so close to each other.

Goldie, self-described submissive

Know the Risks

As with bondage, spanking and any other form of sex game, it's essential that you have a safe word that can be used the second that either of you feels uncomfortable. And it must be adhered to – by both of you. Just as the submissive partner may want to call a halt to proceedings because they're beginning to feel a little too emotionally or physically battered, the dominant partner might feel uncomfortable at pushing their partner's limits beyond a certain point. They might think that they're bad for enjoying inflicting pain on someone that they love, or freak out when they see crop marks on their lover's body or fear in their eyes. In such cases, a good sub should reassure their partner that it's what they want, that they're doing something very special and that it's something for both of them to enjoy. They should remind the Dom/me that the safe word applies to the two of them and can be used at any time, and they should agree that no one will ever be reproached for using it.

In addition to setting your safe word, you should also establish your mutual boundaries before you start your 'scene' (the term used to describe a sub/Dom or other kind of kinky play session), even if you're only playing psychological games rather than indulging in any physical acts.

Indeed, it can be even more important to discuss your limits if you're indulging in erotic emotional abuse, as you won't necessarily know what buttons you could inadvertently press by humiliating your partner: they may love being called a filthy slut but hate being called a bad girl; adore being told that they've got a tiny penis and aren't worthy to service you, but hate being told that they have an ugly face. So it's worth setting mutual guidelines well before play starts and sticking rigidly to them, at least to begin. Once you're familiar with playing humiliation games together, you may be more aware of your partner's positive sexual triggers, at which point you can get more creative with your abuse.

It will really help if you talk about your erotic daydreams and previous experiences before you start playing. Tell your partner what you've fantasised about or tried before and enjoyed, what you've tried and disliked and what your motivations are for liking or disliking certain acts. (**Note**: never say that you loved an experience because your ex was such a talented lover – that way lie jealousy and hurt.) If your partner seems less than willing to open up, say things like, 'So if I did this, would you like it?', 'What would you think if I . . . ?' and 'One day I'd like to . . .'

Once you've decided on exactly what you're going to try, discuss any specific fears that you have relating to the fantasy and talk in detail about what you would and wouldn't like once the game gets started. Tell your partner how far you'd be prepared for it to go, where the areas of flexibility are and what your absolute 'no way' limits are. If one of you is going to be gagged, decide how you are going to communicate the safe word. You may decide to raise a hand to indicate discomfort (assuming your wrists aren't tied) or hold a ball in your hand and drop it if you feel that you want things to stop. Alternatively, you may decide to stand up or hum a tune. It doesn't matter which option you choose, as long as you have a way to indicate that you want things to stop. Playing without a safe word is a sure-fire way to damage your relationship unless (or even if) you're very seasoned players indeed.

As a submissive, you should be prepared to go beyond your comfort zone, as that's where the greatest benefits lie, but only do so a little at a time and *never* do anything that your gut tells you isn't right. A good Dom/me will never try to push their partner to do something they're not comfortable with.

The most important rule of all is to respect each other. Each partner needs to remember to consider the other's needs and desires as much as their own. It's not all about what the Dom/me wants, but neither is it all about getting the submissive to a particular place. If the top gets engrossed in the buzz of control or the bottom gets wrapped up in the pleasure of spacing out, the connection is lost and it becomes a form of masturbation.

Once you've set your guidelines, what you need to do next is decide who's going to be the submissive (or 'bottom') and who's going to be the Dom/me (or 'top') in your first scene. One or both of you may be drawn to a particular role (if you're lucky, one of you will feel hornier at the idea of being dominant while the other will get aroused at the idea of being ordered around). If not, you could toss a coin to decide who's going to be the boss. You can always swap roles afterwards (or even mid-scene) if you find that the role you've assumed doesn't get you off. As with all kinks, it's only by experimenting that you'll know exactly what works for you.

Submit to My Authority

If you're only mildly curious about indulging your submissive side, it may be best to start with non-physical submission and only up the ante once you've got used to the psychological effects that this can bring. While some people feel elated and energised about relinquishing control, others find it distressing or simply plain dull. If you discover that you *do* have a dormant submissive side, which huge numbers of men and women do, there are numerous ways in which to play with it.

Talking dirty

At the mildest level is sub/Dom dirty talk. This could entail nothing more than being called humiliating names such as whore, worm, slut, bastard or 'subby' (a derogatory term for submissive). Alternatively, you can get into a narrative and go into more detail. For example, 'You're such a subby little slut that I bet you'd love to have my cock in your mouth, but I'm not going to let you have it. You're going to have to beg me for it before I deign to let you suck me. And even then I might refuse.' Or, 'You pathetic worm. Call that a cock? I can see you getting hard, but don't think it's coming anywhere near me – you're not worthy. If you're really good, maybe I'll let you touch yourself, but if you come anywhere near me there's going to be trouble.' This type of talk can be used while you're having sex or on its own – you'd be surprised how much of a turn-on it can be for a submissive when someone whispers filth in their ear at a party, where they're unable to act on their arousal.

If you do move on to talking filth during sex, you may actually decide to do the things that are being talked about. This could be as simple as having rough doggy-style sex, while talking about how much the woman loves it hard and deep, or sitting on a man's face and grinding off against his lips and nose so that his breathing is stifled. You can also incorporate slightly crueller aspects into your play, such as hair pulling, face slapping (never strike anywhere near the ear, though as this can pop your partner's ear drum), breast slapping, genital slapping (go gently and remove any rings), biting, scratching or 'making' a partner take large or multiple sex toys inside them or have anal sex.

But remember, you are only simulating doing things against your partner's will. If you use anal sex as 'punishment', for example, you should still follow the standard anal sex rules of starting slowly and gently and using lots of lubricant to avoid causing rips to the anus. However, you can still incorporate humiliation into loving anal sex in a sub/Dom scene. You might start off by performing analingus on your partner, and tell them what a cheap whore or pathetic worm they are for loving having their arse licked. (But use a dental dam to avoid getting nasty diseases; even if you've both had full STI tests, you can still get E-coli and other unpleasant infections from unprotected rimming.) A woman could take a man with a strap-on because he 'only deserves to be taken like a woman'. (Yes, that does have faint misogynistic overtones, but it *is* a woman taking a man up the arse so all in all, it balances.) Or either partner could pretend that they're only having anal sex with their partner because they don't want to give them any pleasure.

Dressed to submit

Of course, submission doesn't just have to take place while you're actually having sex. If you decide that you'd like to play with the idea in other ways, wearing a partner's choice of outfit is a good place to start. The classic item of slave clothing is the collar, signifying that the 'slave' is 'owned' by their partner. These come in numerous varieties from pink fake-fur lined leatherette to intimidating-looking spiked metal collars.

However, you don't have to wear a collar to show your devotion to your Master or Mistress. You could do something as simple as wearing underwear of your partner's choice. Ramping things up a gear, you might go out wearing a short skirt with no underwear, get dressed up in drag (which can work equally well for women as men – see *9½ Weeks* for a hot example) or wearing a cock ring under your jeans. (But never wear a cock ring for more than an hour as it can cause damage.)

At the more extreme end of the spectrum you could even wear a chastity device. These are available for both men and women and vary in levels of extremity. Some completely cover the genitals, while others allow very limited access or come complete with a butt plug or dildo attachment. The Dom/me then decides exactly how long their partner should be chaste for, and may choose to make things harder for them by talking dirty or masturbating in front of them, knowing that it will probably be exquisite agony for the 'slave' as they can't get any satisfaction. You can even get cock cages with spikes inside them that dig into a man every time he gets an erection, or attach a lock to appropriate genital piercings; these are both best left to extreme players only!

TALES FROM THE SCENE: MY PIERCINGS FORM A GREAT CHASTITY BELT

I have three piercings: a Prince Albert and two rings through my scrotum sack. As a consequence, a small padlock can be attached to the rings on my cock and ball sack, which effectively works as a simple and elegant male chastity belt. It's easy to keep clean, and, as long as the padlock is supported by briefs, under normal circumstances, you hardly know it's there. One of the thrilling aspects of this form of pervery is that it can be worn under jeans, shorts, even a business suit, and no one is any the wiser!

The most obvious use of chastity belts is to control a partner's sexual activity, or to hand over your sexual autonomy to that special person in your life. While illicit infidelity may not be a concern in most couples' sex lives, it can add an extra frisson at swingers' parties if the bloke has to ask permission from his significant other before he can be unlocked. This kind of ritual, as well as being sexy, can help to reinforce the bond between primary partners, enhancing the sense that this is something you're doing together rather than apart. But the greatest application of male chastity belts is in stopping masturbation! Nothing feeds desire more than prohibition. After a few nights in a belt, he's bound to be gagging for some action – and all that pent-up sexual energy can be very exciting for everyone involved.

There are some inevitable drawbacks of male chastity belts. Unwanted erections become an uncomfortable ordeal, while serving as a reminder of enforced celibacy. This does become a problem in the morning, when many men experience erections which have nothing to do with sexual desire. When this happens, I often have to endure a six o' clock wake up call, which is particularly painful!

Clearly, those thinking of experimenting with this kind of orgasm control might be reluctant to submit themselves to genital piercing. But there are a number of male chastity belts on the market, the most famous of which is the CB6000. This consists of a lightweight plastic sheath which goes over the penis, and is held in place by being locked to a plastic ring behind the scrotum. Enforced chastity will not be for everyone, but those prepared to experiment can find it an extremely sexy form of power play.

Gary, 31, professor

Playing the slave

If being submissive really turns you on, you may decide to spend a whole evening or weekend as your partner's slave. (There *are* people who maintain sub/Dom roles all the time, known as 24/7 – which stands for twenty-four hours of the day, seven days per week – but, from what I've seen, it isn't really healthy and can often be used to mask destructive relationships.) When it comes to what you actually do during this time, that's up to you and your partner. The submissive might only be allowed to speak when spoken to, or have to keep their eyes downcast at all times. They might be forced to assume certain positions, kneeling on all fours as their partner's footrest or crouching for long periods (a killer on the thighs), ready to perform oral sex on their partner at any time. They may only be allowed to use the toilet in front of their partner or have to ask permission to do anything at all. Or they might simply have to have sex on command. The levels, as ever, are entirely up to you and can be as mild or as wild as you want.

If you're planning on spending any serious length of time submitting to your partner, it's worth establishing a slave contract together, outlining the slave's responsibilities when indulging in play (search the Internet for numerous examples). That way, you both know what you're getting into and can negotiate levels outside the scene, allowing yourself to get fully immersed in the experience once it starts.

There's no such thing as being a 'bad' slave, as long as you do whatever it is that has been mutually agreed between you and your partner. Anyone who describes you as a bad slave for not doing something that you haven't agreed to, or for using a safe word, is wrong and dangerous to play with, so best avoided.

TALES FROM THE SCENE: JUST SAY NO

The man who introduced me to BDSM was called Si. He had a 'full-time' girlfriend called Lucy, but both he and Lucy had secondary relationships, and I was Si's 'part-time' sub. For a year or so, we met up once or twice a month and played; usually he'd tie me up and spank or flog me and then we'd have sex. It was great fun and we started to feel really close to each other.

After a year or so, we decided to push things further. He wanted to formally 'slave train' me, following some suggestions he'd read in a book called *SM 101*. I was a bit wary, but agreed to try it. We hired a dungeon for a couple of hours and planned everything in advance, including the safe word. For the first hour we did our usual play; I bent over a bench and he spanked me, then used a cane on me and then a flogger.

Then we moved on to the new part of the game, which involved me kneeling naked at Si's feet and following a series of orders. At first it was fine. I followed all his commands, called him 'Master' and felt quite comfortable with it. But then he told me to crawl on my knees towards where he sat in a chair, take out his cock and suck it. I immediately felt humiliated, like I was being used, rather than treated like someone he cared about. I hated the idea of letting him down, hated the idea that I wasn't a 'proper' sub and desperately didn't want to waste the very expensive dungeon time. But I also knew that if I forced myself to do something that made me feel this bad, I'd risk hurting myself and spoiling our relationship.

'I'm really sorry,' I said. 'I think I'm going to have to say the safe word.'

He looked at me for a minute, obviously confused. 'OK, say it then,' he answered, finally.

I said the safe word, then burst into tears. I thought he'd be angry or hurt, but he wasn't. He hugged me, comforted me and asked me what had gone wrong. We were both surprised by what had happened, as I'd never had a reaction like that before. We realised that I just didn't feel comfortable being at 'slave' level with him. He said, 'I'm just not the right Master for you,' which I denied at the time, but have since decided was probably right. I've realised that in order to be comfortable with that level of submission, I need to feel that I can totally trust and depend on my partner, and Si didn't fit into that category.

Goldie, self-described submissive

One thing that is generally frowned upon is 'topping from the bottom' whereby the 'slave' instructs the Dom/me as to what they want done to them. This not only reverses the roles of the play (although it's a commonly held belief in fetish circles that the sub is actually the one in control as they have the power to stop the 'scene' at any point and the Dom/me must oblige, whereas the Dom/me is a lot less likely to, even though they're just as free to make that choice), but also denies the sub the chance to surrender fully to their partner's whims. And that's what being a true submissive is about.

TRUE CONFESSIONS
I MAKE MY SUB DO WHATEVER I CAN'T

Having the painters in used to be a euphemism for having your period. For me, it means calling a sub in to do the things for me that I can't!

I love spending time pleasuring myself. It's one of life's joys, and why on earth women shy away from something so fabulous beats me. Perhaps I had overdone it a bit, but I developed RSI in my thumb – laugh all you want to, but this was serious.

I went to see my doctor to check it didn't need treatment. He got straight to the point, asking what I had been doing. 'Painting,' I told him, and in part that was true; I have recently taken up drawing and painting, and let's face it, who's going to own up to wanking so much to a strange doctor? He didn't believe me and smiled as he told me I'd need to stop for a month. I squeaked and he nodded, explaining that without rest now I may permanently damage my thumb and not be able to paint again. I swear I nearly passed out.

Chastened, I headed home. Yes, I could revert to vibrators, but it's the personal touch that works best for me. I logged on to my email account in an attempt to divert myself and found an email from a sub called Lucca. Was there any service he could offer Mistress? A manicure? Carrying bags? Footstool? An idea began to form.

Twenty minutes later a rosy-cheeked Lucca was at my front door, a bunch of flowers in one hand and chocolates in the other. 'Mistress needs some painting done?' I smiled as I pulled him in to explain his duty.

Lucca proved to be an excellent painter. This may be shocking to some, to use a man as some kind of human sex toy, but consider this: my needs were generously met and Lucca, a natural submissive, gained satisfaction from giving me satisfaction. You've got to love a win–win, haven't you?

Mistress Grace, Domme

Dominant Demands

As a Dom/me, you need to have an awareness of exactly what kind of submission your partner is into. In addition to clear communication, an important part of it is reading your partner's responses. Are they wriggling around when you hit them because they're in pain or because they want you to punish them for being 'bad'? Although it can take time to learn, it's well worth paying attention to, as it will make your sessions much more fluid.

TIPS FROM THE SCENE

Communication is most important during a scene, especially if the bottom is being restrained or pain is being inflicted. The top needs to be constantly on the lookout for signs that the bottom isn't physically OK. Once the endorphins get flowing, a bottom can drift off into a trance, and it's easy for the top to assume that's what's happened, when in fact, they've passed out (I've seen this happen several times in clubs, so it is a real risk). The risk of fainting is high if someone's hands are tied above their head – I once saw a girl pass out and nearly choke to death in this position because her collar had caught on the equipment behind her and all her weight was on her neck.

If the bottom is gagged, one way of checking is to grab their hand and squeeze twice. If the bottom squeezes back twice, they're OK. Otherwise, untie them immediately. People can think these rules are silly, but you'd be amazed how easy it is for something to go wrong and it's just not worth it.

Aside from checking physical safety, it's also important to check a bottom is emotionally OK. A good top knows when to push and when to hold back, and you can only learn that through talking and watching. Some bottoms like to be humiliated, for example called names like 'slut' during scenes; others hate it, but most bottoms won't stop a scene until they've been pushed quite a long way, so the top has to watch the bottom's face and see what the reaction is. You might be able to get away with pushing a bottom further than they want to go once, but it's unlikely they'll come back for more. Telling a bottom how well they're doing ('good girl' and 'good boy' are extremely powerful phrases) is a great thing to do.

And finally, talking afterwards is the best way you have of making sure it's even better next time. What worked? What didn't? What do you want to try again? By talking before, during and after you're both a lot more likely to come back for more.

Goldie, self-described submissive

However, the Dom/me's role is also about pushing their partner's limits – gently – to give them the sexual high that being 'out of control' can bring. That doesn't mean ignoring the safe word, but it may entail asking them to do something on the outer regions of their comfort zone: acts that they are only into very occasionally, but which, as your submissive, they might indulge in because they 'have to'.

Orgasm control

If you and your partner enjoy sub/Dom dirty talk, you may want to experiment with orgasm training. Although this can take a fair bit of time to master, it's not that complicated. To start with, when you're indulging in sex play, tell your partner that they're not allowed to climax until you tell them to. This may well initially have the opposite effect because the brain is a contrary thing, and if someone is submissive, being told what *not* to do can be a total turn-on, in the hope that they'll get punished. However, with a little practice you should be able to take your partner right to the edge of orgasm, then keep them teetering there – well, for as long as you want. And the longer you make them wait, the more intense their eventual orgasm will be.

Once you've got your partner used to controlling their orgasm, you can start setting them targets: take them right to the edge, then tell them that they have to come within a count of ten and start stimulating them in the way that they most enjoy (for example, oral sex – use your fingers to count down). If they don't climax in time, stop and tell them that they don't deserve to come. Although this is intensely frustrating, it can be a massive turn-on for a true sub. To make things harder on them, once you've banned them from coming, you could masturbate in front of them, put on some porn or simply leave the room, having told them they're not allowed to touch themselves.

Repeat this until your partner can come to your countdown on a reliable basis. Once you've got to that stage, it's simply a case of giving them less and less physical stimulation each time you start your countdown, until they become aroused simply on hearing you say, '10 . . . 9 . . . 8 . . .' and climax when you get to '1' without any contact at all.

At that stage, you can take your game out and about: whisper a countdown into their ear when you're in the pub; phone them up at work and say nothing, other than the countdown; or order them to phone a friend, then mouth the countdown once their friend picks up the phone. You'll be amazed how many orgasms you can give your partner without touching them.

Another way to exercise orgasm control is by limiting the number of orgasms your partner is allowed to have during a 'scene' (if they're allowed to come at all), or by making them earn the right to climax by carrying out whatever humiliating task you set them. However, orgasm control should, as with any other kind of sub/Dom play, be consensual and not simply an excuse to be a lazy lover.

Pain play

Another facet of sub/Dom play is pain play. If pain forms an integral part of your sex play, the person who likes being hurt would be described as a masochist and the person who enjoys administering the pain a sadist. (The former is named for Leopold Von Sacher Masoch, author of the seminal submissive novel *Venus in Furs*, while the latter is for the frankly, rather scary Marquis de Sade.)

Hair pulling, scratching and biting are all ways of incorporating pain and they can all release endorphins in the same way that spanking does (see Chapter Five). And then there's the world of whips, crops, floggers and canes. These come in at various levels, from rubber whips and mild floggers made from horse hair that can provide a sting but won't actually break the skin, to leather cat-o'-nine-tails that shouldn't really be brought into play without going on a sub/Dom training course, as they can cause major damage if used in the wrong way.

If you don't want to go on a training course, the safest way forward is to pick something at the milder end of the scale, avoid hitting the kidneys, face, neck or joints and focus your attention on fleshy areas such as the buttocks and thighs. Start gently and work your way up slowly as with spanking, and, as ever, have a safe word. Agree beforehand if you're allowed to break the skin (should you want to) and if you do go for that option, never use your toys with multiple partners as this can spread infection. And make sure that you clean the wounds (and the crop, whip or flogger) with antibacterial wipes afterwards to avoid infection.

Nipple clamps are another fun way to throw some pain into the mix. Again, these come in various 'strengths', with some offering a mild pinch, while others are adjustable and capable of inflicting a lot of pain. Start with something gentle, and do bear in mind that the most painful part of nipple clamping is when the clamps are removed and blood rushes back into the area. As such, you should never take someone to their maximum pain threshold when clamping them, as removing the clamps can send them over the edge. A milder alternative to clamps are clip-on earrings or plastic clothes pegs, either of which can offer a similar kick without you having to buy any specialist equipment.

However, there's no need to buy any equipment at all if you want to inflict pain on your partner. With a bit of creativity, you can find some perfectly good punishment tools in your own back yard.

TALES FROM THE SCENE: *A STINGING PUNISHMENT*

I love going to female domination clubs, and I have vivid memories of one particular night. I was after a particular sub who had caused me inconvenience some years before. This boy had tightened my corset on arrival at a club, but had mischievously tied the cord in a double knot instead of bow. Once home, I found I was stuck. The corset was so tight that I couldn't undo or loosen it. I couldn't even sleep in it. I took the only path open to me and called on my local firemen. Oddly enough, even at 4 a.m., they were soon all awake and keen to help me out of my corset. Remember, ladies, that if you ever get in a pickle they really are the most adorable men.

I made a note of the event in my black book. I pride myself on making my 'scenes' at clubs memorable. I adopt a soft and slightly deeper voice when I'm playing. For me, it's far more powerful than shouting; it means the sub has to lean in to hear what I am saying and at that point is already under my direction. It's never a good sign when I go quiet, and it makes me laugh to think how often it's mistaken for caring. Until the pain starts that is!

This particular night, I had gone for an all-black costume, complemented with a scarlet corset, black rubber gloves, thumb screws (these are wider and more versatile than nipple clamps) and a sheath of nettles; fresh from a friend's garden and of the English variety, these offer a particularly unpleasant sting. The good news with nettles is that they freeze well so can be used all year round.

Think of them as the punishment that just keeps on giving.

Bless him, the errant boy had no idea and was soon bound, naked, over a table. We attracted a large circle of voyeurs, as I stroked him all around his boyhood and bum with the nettles. The dirty boy loved it. Oh, I am sure it hurt, but not lastingly – that would be wrong – and I know he will never tie a double knot without thinking of me. And that's what it's all about, after all.

Mistress Grace, Domme

Watersports

Another way to get Dom/me on your partner without spending any money is by, err, spending a penny. Although the mere idea of watersports may make some people go 'Yuk', there's actually very little risk. Urine is sterile when it comes out of the body, so as long as you don't store it to play with at a later date (which is, let's face it, a little extreme), you won't suffer any symptoms from indulging in golden showers. (There is a minimal risk of passing on STIs through watersports, but as long as you've both been tested, avoid drinking urine and getting it in open wounds, you're pretty safe.)

Passing water is something that we're trained to keep private from the time that we're potty-trained. As such, even something as simple as having to urinate in front of someone else may be humiliating for a submissive. If you're already one of those couples that happily pees in front of each other, you may decide to take things to the next level and make your partner urinate in the bath or shower, so that you can see it flowing out of them. Or you might decide to urinate *on* your partner (again, the bath or shower is best for this, otherwise you have to put down a lot of newspapers, plastic sheets and towels first to avoid turning your house into a urinal).

At more extreme levels still, you may decide you want to urinate over your partner's face and/or make them swallow it. If you do opt for this, be kind and drink a lot of water first. Lager can also help, as it makes it easier to pee (alcohol being a diuretic). Basically, your urine should be clear or as close to clear as possible (which it should be anyway if you're properly hydrated); if not it can contain excessive iodine which may make your partner ill, not to mention tasting utterly vile.

Whether you choose to indulge in verbal humiliation, pain play, watersports or some devious game of your own creation, there's no need to feel bad about dominating a partner as long as it's consensual. Indeed, being the dominant partner can be a lot harder work than being submissive, if you really get into it, so if anything, you're doing a submissive partner a favour by treating them mean.

Hitting the Switch

Of course, there's nothing to say that one of you need always be the dominant partner and the other submissive. Taking it in turns with your partner to be the one who is in control can be a lot of fun. Some people even switch mid-scene, going from being roughly penetrated to forcing their partner to go down on them; or overpowering their partner during a play fight and taking full advantage of their position.

Beyond the safety guidelines, there are no rules to govern the way in which you play, so just do what comes naturally and you may be surprised at some of the things that turn you on. And remember, if you don't like something, all you need do is use the safe word and stop it in an instant, so there's no harm in a bit of experimentation.

Switching helps to keep a sense of balance in your relationship, it allows both of you to experience the joys of both submission and domination and it also keeps you in check when you're Domming your partner because you know that it won't be long before they're punishing you.

TRUE CONFESSIONS
WE PUSHED EACH OTHER TO THE LIMITS

I was bored with my usual social life, so one night a naughty friend of mine took me to a fetish club. I felt at home and soon I was a regular there. I'd go there on my own, dressed in my sluttiest outfit, and always go home with someone on my arm – sometimes two people.

Before long, I'd learned a lot about the sub/Dom scene and loved both sides of it: having a man trembling on his knees before me while I ordered him to lick my boots or kiss my arse; being shagged hard by a muscular guy after he'd given me a thorough spanking, knowing full well that when he'd finished he was going to make me suck his cock; or ordering a gorgeous woman to lick me while her boyfriend had sex with me. OK, so maybe it was a bit extreme, but I was making up for lost time.

The night that I met Karl, I was with a guy and a girl who I was having a three-way relationship with, but I still ended up having a long conversation with him about sex. He described himself as a Dom and I got into an argument with him about whether it was healthy to be purely dominant rather than switch. He said that he could never find submission the slightest bit sexy, which made me think that he'd never been dominated by someone who knew what they were doing. I could tell that he fancied me, and I felt the same way about him – which is exactly why I left him at the club and went home with my two lovers, having got him really turned on by describing some of the more submissive things I'd got up to. He'd got my number, and I didn't want to make things too easy for him; I wanted him to come round to my way of thinking.

There then followed a power game for a month or so, with him calling to ask me out and me agreeing, only to have him cancel at the last minute and vice versa. We'd already entered into sub/Dom play, even though neither of us would admit it. Eventually, and after a few filthy instant messenger sessions, we agreed on a time and a place and both turned up. He confessed that he had a girlfriend who he was faithful to even though she wasn't kinky. I asked if he was in love with her, and mocked him for being weak when he confessed that he wasn't and that he was only staying with her because she was pretty and looked good on his arm. He told me that his kinks were domination, women in glasses and the taste of a woman. I went to the toilet, came back with a hand that was sopping wet, wiped it over his face and said, 'Two out of three ain't bad.' He ordered a cab and asked for my address when it arrived without even checking first if it was OK to go back to my place. I gave the address but made him pay for the cab. Once we were at the flat, both of us were stupidly horny, but neither of us would make a move; we each wanted the other to be first to acquiesce.

In the end, alcohol did the job for us. After a bottle of wine, we were all over each other by mutual desire: I genuinely can't remember who made the first move and neither can he. When we got to the bedroom it was another matter though. He punished me for teasing him and making him wait. He spanked me, called me a whore, pulled my hair, slapped my face – and I loved it. But once we'd had hard, nasty sex, I made him go down on me and treat me like a goddess. It felt like a match of equals and we both gave as good as we got. I had the raunchiest sex I'd ever had and I still think about it to this day, even though outside the bedroom there sadly wasn't enough to keep us together.

Jemma, 45, self-described switch

Are You Ready For More?

You may well be almost completely kink-conversant by now, with a host of fetish outfits and toys to add spice to your sex life, a well-stocked porn collection, a social life that involves lap-dancing clubs, fetish nights and orgasm control down the pub, as well as being informed about the numerous ways in which to punish your partner (or be punished). But maybe you still feel that something is lacking in your sex life? Perhaps one partner just isn't enough? If so, it could be that threesomes, orgies and swinging are for you. So, pack your condoms and lube, and prepare yourself for the world of group sex.

CHAPTER EIGHT

Group Sex

Once upon a time, the words 'group sex' conjured up images of 1970s swingers picking car keys out of bowls before shagging their neighbour's wife, whether they fancied her or not. Even at the time, this stereotype was far from accurate, but in recent years, group sex has seen a massive image change. Threesomes and moresomes seemed to go hand in hand with the ecstasy generation; the rise of lipstick lesbianism and the bicurious babe has led to thousands of women persuading their (generally less-than-reticent) lovers to let them invite another woman into the bed; and sex parties, as depicted in the film *Shortbus*, are now happening in pretty much every major city. There are even designer orgies in which people are vetted to ensure they're good-looking enough before they're allowed to attend. In short, group sex has become stylish.

However, just because something sexual is in vogue (or indeed, in *Vogue*), that doesn't mean that you have to do it. There's absolutely nothing wrong with having group sex, but it's something you should only enter into if both you and your partner are equally enthusiastic. While the fantasy can be extremely hot, if one partner is unsure, it's unwise (and unkind) to pressure them into trying it. You're more likely to find jealousy arising and it could even lead to the end of your relationship.

If, on the other hand, you are both keen on the idea, group sex can be a fabulous way to alleviate jealousy, as nothing is happening behind your partner's back, and there can be less of a fear of infidelity because both of you are getting your kicks from shagging other people within the boundaries of your relationship.

'Apart from the obvious attraction of being able to be open about having sex with multiple partners, group sex can help you and your partner to find a new kind of deeper trust, love and affection.'

Ashley Hames, TV presenter and sexual explorer

There are numerous ways in which you can explore your fantasies about getting frisky with multiple partners. You might hunt someone out for a threesome and enjoy having another man or woman in your bed. Or, if your group-sex fantasies run more to the 'cast of thousands' end of the spectrum, there are websites full of adverts from people seeking others to join them for all manner of debauched play from gang bangs to dogging (having sex in cars while other people watch and join in). You might find that partner-swapping is more to your taste, or you could decide that an organised event is what you're after.

Generally, there's far less of a taboo around approaching third (fourth, fifth and sixth) parties for some hot action than there was ten years ago, and there is certainly a host of benefits that group sex can offer your relationship.

TALES FROM THE SCENE: *IT TAKES ALL SORTS*

There are many different aspects to group sex, which can be appreciated in many different ways for many different reasons. To do any of these things you have to have an outgoing sexuality. Beyond that, different types of group sex serve different purposes. A threesome conducted privately can be incredibly intimate and very much about the couple themselves. Swinging can be about female bisexuality; a Dom/sub relationship where one partner 'gives' the other to someone else; showing off your partner; preventing a relationship from growing stale; letting a less experienced partner catch up; or it needn't be about 'group' sex at all. Gang bangs and *bukkake* (being ejaculated on by multiple men at the same time) obviously fulfil an extraordinary need of the women involved, but can also build male bonding. Group sex brings multiple physical sensations but there is also the delight of taboo-breaking. In fact the sex-in-the-head high from group sex can actually be greater than the physical side, as that can overwhelm the senses. Speaking personally, the best thing about group sex has always been women enjoying themselves in ways that so much of society still feels they never should.

Mark Roberts, organising secretary of Fever swinging events

No matter what sort of group romp you're after, it's surprisingly easy to find what you desire as long as you know where to look. But before you fire up that Internet connection, it's worth sitting down with your partner to discuss whether it's something that you really want to do, and familiarise yourself with the potential hazards. While thousands of people have very happy group sex, either as a one-off or on a regular basis, it's not something to enter into lightly.

Know the Risks

While group sex can be incredibly appealing in fantasy, when it comes to actually living it out you need to be fully prepared for how it could make you feel. While everything may well go seamlessly when you think about it in theory, in practice there's always a danger that messy real-life emotions will spill out, so that your turn-on becomes a trauma.

You might feel jealous watching your partner climax with another man or woman with just the same intensity that they climax with you. Conversely, you might find yourself feeling hurt because your partner doesn't exhibit any jealousy, but instead gets aroused when he or she sees you being caressed by another person. The third party might feel uncomfortable if you treat them like a spare part, there purely to service your needs (which is impolite, to say the least, unless you're having sex with a submissive and that's part of your scene). Or you might find that one or both of you develops an attachment to the new addition to your sex life (though if both of you feel the same way, there's nothing to stop you from going for an open relationship and indulging your mutual desires). It could even be that once you get down to it, only one of you actually fancies the third party, and the other feels left out because they can't get fully involved.

So, as ever, it is essential that you sit down and establish ground rules with your partner before you find that new addition or go to a sex party. Decide whether you'll pick people to play with together or whether you're each allowed to choose your own 'targets' and invite them to join the pair of you. Discuss what you both think is acceptable. It may be that you agree to simply go to a sex party together and observe in the first instance, making friends and familiarising yourself with the group scene. You might choose to have sex in front of other people and only involve them in what you're doing if both of you feel relaxed. You might decide that touching someone of the same gender is acceptable but touching someone of the opposite sex isn't. Or you could set yourself sexual limits: you're allowed to kiss and caress other people but penetrative sex is something that you'll keep just for yourselves.

'Don't be afraid to watch. You can go to a sex party and not have sex if you prefer to just watch, at least for the big ones. Maybe later on you'll want to participate.'

Annie Sprinkle, ex-prostitute and porn star and PhD sexologist

As usual, there's no right or wrong, and it's simply down to what you feel comfortable with. However, always err on the side of caution: if one of you is happy with your group romp being a 'free for all', but the other wants it to be more of an exploratory thing, stick to the stricter guidelines. Group sex is supposed to enhance your relationship, not damage it, and although it's not for everyone, the happiest couples who have group sex are those who've talked through all the options at length, agreed their own boundaries and stuck to them rigorously. You can always change the ground rules at a later date and have another group experience, if you realise you can push your limits further than you initially set them. However, it's much harder to get your relationship back on track if you've pushed yourselves to the max and found that you're not comfortable seeing your partner with another person, after all.

Even if you think that you're both able to control your jealousy enough to watch each other engaged in sexual acts with other people, there are other issues to bear in mind. Increasing the number of partners in a sexual situation fairly obviously increases the risk of spreading STIs. As such, it's essential to only practise safer sex (including not sharing sex toys, unless they're covered in a condom) when you indulge in group acts, which may mean that reality is much more limiting than your fantasy.

Then there are the more mundane practicalities of the matter. If you live in a small town, it may be worth travelling to a nearby city for your swinging initiation: the last thing you want to do is start getting it on in front of a crowd, only to realise that you're being watched by your kids' primary school teacher, your next-door neighbour or your mum.

You should also bear in mind that just because you like the idea of having group sex, it doesn't mean that your dream third party is magically going to appear, find both people they're expected to play with attractive, have a similar idea about the kind of sex that should happen and leave afterwards without any complications. Similarly, you can't always guarantee discretion. It makes sense to spend time waiting for the perfect person, rather than rushing to accept the first offer that comes along (and you can guarantee that once you start looking in earnest, the offers will come in).

When you invite a third party into your sex life, you are opening the door to a host of emotional issues, and that may well be a risk that you're prepared to take for the sexual pleasures that group sex can bring. Just make sure that you enter into it with your eyes wide open though, and you'll be a lot more likely to have a good time.

Group Sex for Two

Given the potential issues that can arise, some people decide that it's better to keep their group-sex fantasies in their mind. And with just a little imagination, it's easy enough to simulate a group-sex scene without getting anyone else involved. You just need to spend a little time planning your evening.

There are numerous props and aids that you can use to help create the idea that there's another man or woman involved in your bedroom antics. Sex toys are the obvious place to start. Judicious use of a blindfold along with a phallic toy or two and ideally some lube will make it easier for a woman to imagine she's being pleasured by two or more men at once. Conversely, a vaginal or anal sheath toy such as a Tenga or Fleshlight can be very convincing, particularly if the woman blindfolds the man or sits on his face to mask his vision while using it.

But group sex is about more than mere genitals. To truly create the mood, you should get as many senses involved as possible. Wear one type of perfume or aftershave and spray another unfamiliar type on to the other pillow, so that your partner can imagine that they can smell the third party. Play some pornography in the background, or even record your own orgasmic moans then play them back, so you can hear stereo sex sound effects. Try wearing a leather glove on one hand, chilling one hand in a bowl of iced water or painting the nails on one hand only, so that your partner feels as if they have two people's hands stroking them. If you use different sexual techniques from those you normally would, your partner will find it easier to imagine there's someone new touching them, and if you can use different rhythms with both hands (even if it does feel like rubbing your stomach while patting your head) then so much the better.

All your partner then needs do to complete the picture is close their eyes, float into their erotic daydreams and – ideally – tell you exactly what they can feel being done to them. And, of course, once your partner has been pleasured with a fictional group-sex session, you might decide that it's your turn to lie back and be the centre of attention. Even if you don't like the idea of having sex with multiple partners, being stroked all over and stimulated through caresses of multiple erogenous zones at once is something that everyone should try at least once.

Three's a Crowd

If you and your partner are equally intrigued by the idea of a group romp, have discussed your ground rules and agreed what you want to do, and have a big stack of condoms and dental dams, there's no reason for you not to make your dreams come true.

The easiest place to start in terms of group sex is with a threesome. Every new person you add to the sexual equation adds a new dynamic, so it's best to get used to having one more person to accommodate before moving on to multiples.

One of the most common fantasies shared by men and women is that of having a threesome with two women and one man (otherwise known as FFM, standing for two females and a male). Many women are bicurious, so they can satisfy their sapphic cravings by indulging in a three-way; and men innately want variety, so a threesome with a partner and another woman is a way to satisfy that craving without actually being unfaithful. Many men also enjoy watching lesbian sex, so it's something that can work on multiple levels.

However, MMF (work it out!) threesomes are also a common fantasy. Some men get off on the idea of being cuckolded, while some women like the idea of having both ends filled at once in a classic 'spit-roast' style (so named because a woman with a penis in her mouth and her vagina or anus resembles a pig being spit-roasted), or enjoying anal sex and vaginal sex at the same time courtesy of a DP (double penetration) session.

TALES FROM THE SCENE: *EXPLORE YOURSELF FULLY*

For an individual, group sex is a very intense form of physical joy. But it's also an emotional high because it's very affirming of your desirability. For a couple, a great group-sex experience can fuel fantasies between them for weeks and months afterwards, so it enriches their one-on-one experiences. It validates their partner choice by proving that other people find their partner very attractive. And it deepens their private bond by sharing a taboo experience that can't be told to many people. For bisexual women, it allows them to experience sex with the opposite gender to their partner without excluding that partner. This is really very important. Bisexual women are probably the most suppressed of the big sexual minorities in the country today. Bisexual men can easily have sex with men through the very well-developed gay scene. But bisexual women are often held in low regard by lesbians who often feel they cannot be trusted emotionally, and sometimes even resent the way they live apparently conventional lives, avoiding the difficulties of being an 'out' gay woman.

Mark Roberts, organising secretary of Fever swinging events

Finding your third party

Although it may be tempting to invite a friend to join you for a threesome, it is most likely to lead to trouble. Any jealousy could damage the friendship, and you may feel that you have to choose between your partner and your friend. In addition, if you feel uncomfortable after the ménage à trois, it can be less than ideal having to see the third party out and about in your social life.

An infinitely better option is to either go out on the pull together and find a stranger to seduce (if the female partner approaches the woman, it's generally a lot more likely to work) or use one of the numerous adult dating websites to find a third party.

Do be warned that people aren't always inclined to be

honest online, so when you're first arranging to meet a potential threesome mate, never suggest meeting them at your home or local pub, but instead choose a neutral location where no one knows you (or the person you're playing with). And although it can be tempting to dive right in once you've found someone who's willing to join you in the bedroom, it's far better to take a little time getting to know the person first, to establish that they are as happy with the idea as you are and, to be blunt, aren't likely to turn into a bunny boiler or stalker. By spending time chatting to your potential third party over email and phone, you can establish mutual ground rules and discuss what you'd like to do together so that you're all on the same page when you finally meet up. Use your gut instinct too: if you don't feel comfortable, even if you can't figure out why, don't meet up. There are plenty of people out there willing to play and it's better to take your time and be safe.

TRUE CONFESSIONS
WE SHARED A LOVER

When I first met my boyfriend, Jack, we were both quite young and inexperienced, so when we saw a documentary about group sex a few years into our relationship, we both admitted that it was something we both wanted to try. Jack had had a few partners before we got together, but I'd only had one, and even though I loved Jack to bits, I didn't like the idea of marrying him before I'd had a bit more experience. Group sex seemed to be a good way to experiment without us having to break up.

I'd always wondered what it would be like to have sex with a woman, so we decided to have a threesome with another woman to start with. Jack's a bit of a geek, so he searched the Internet and found a website where we could post an advert for the kind of person we wanted. I've got quite small boobs, so I wanted someone who was more well endowed. However, I didn't want Jack to fancy the other woman more than he fancied me, so I specified that it had to be a brunette: Jack's got a big thing about blondes and was so into seeing me with another woman that he was prepared to agree to anything I asked.

We had a fair few replies that went nowhere: several people refused to send us pictures and we didn't want to meet someone without seeing what they looked like first. A few of them were illiterate, and I wanted someone we could talk to first, so that ruled them out. And I'm sure that a couple of them were men, because the pictures they sent looked like they were ripped out of a magazine. But after about a month we got an email from Carin, who seemed perfect. She was twenty-six – a year older than me – and her picture showed a pretty girl with long, curly, dark hair, a sweet smile and a sexy figure. She was wearing a summer dress in the picture rather than underwear, which made me more convinced that she was genuine.

We arranged to meet her at a pub in the centre of town. On the night, I was nervous and got a bit emotional, bursting into tears just before we left because I was worried that Jack would prefer her to me. He cuddled me and said we didn't have to do anything that I didn't want to and that we could cancel if I wanted, but that seemed unfair on Carin. We'd agreed over email that we'd just talk at first, and no one was under any obligation to do anything. She seemed as nervous as me because she'd never been with a woman before, so I decided that we'd go ahead.

When we arrived, we couldn't find Carin, so we ordered ourselves drinks and sat down at a table near the door, so we'd be easy to spot. Every time the door opened my heart leaped into my throat and, after a few guys had come in, I finally recognised Carin from her photo. I smiled at her and, a little shyly, she came over to our table and asked if we were Jack and Aly. We said yes, and I went to the bar with her to get her a drink, leaving Jack sitting alone.

She apologised for being late and explained that she'd been standing outside wondering whether she could go through with it. 'I've never done anything like this before,' she said.

I told her that I'd been just as nervous, which seemed to relax her, and by the time we got back to Jack, we were chatting comfortably. At first we just talked about music and TV but after a couple of glasses of wine, Carin said, 'You're both even better in real life than you were in your photos. We could go back to yours if you want.'

Jack and I exchanged a look and I told her that'd be lovely.

Once we were back at home, we sat around, not sure what to do. Eventually Jack piped up, 'Why don't you two kiss?'

Carin and I looked at each other for a bit, then she moved towards me. When our lips met, it felt really gentle and sweet, just as I'd imagined it would, and things seemed to follow naturally from there. Carin and I petted each other and then she pulled my top off to kiss my boobs. Jack undid his trousers and stroked himself as he watched us. I was getting really wet from kissing Carin and soon we were both naked and playing with each other. I used my fingers on her – I'd told her that I wasn't sure I could go down on her, but she was OK with that – and she rubbed her thigh against me as I did, so I could feel my orgasm building up. She came around my fingers after about fifteen minutes which was a huge ego boost: I'd worried that I might not be able to please a woman because it was such a new thing.

It seemed unfair that Jack was being ignored so I beckoned him over and started to suck him as Carin recovered. 'Can I have a go?' Carin asked after a few minutes. I felt a brief pang of jealousy, but she'd told me she wasn't interested in running off with Jack and just wanted a wild experience, so I pulled away and let her take my place. It felt odd seeing Jack with Carin but he started to kiss me and that made me feel better.

Jack came with Carin, then she and I played with each other while he got hard again. 'I'd like to see him shag you,' Carin said, once Jack was ready, and I felt a flutter at the idea of her watching us. Jack slid inside me and Carin played with herself as we had sex. It took me a long time to come and when I did, it wasn't that intense because I felt self-conscious. However, when Carin went down on me afterwards I came really noisily.

Afterwards, we got dressed and had another glass of wine before ordering Carin a cab. We'd agreed it was going to be a one-off – I didn't like the idea of Jack having sex with anyone else regularly – but I'm glad that we did it that once. Jack and I often talk about that night now, and even though we haven't had group sex since, I wouldn't rule it out in the future.

Aly, 27, shop manager

What to ask a potential third party

When you find someone who you think could fit the bill, ask them the following questions:

- Do you have any STIs?

- Are there any specific areas where you do/don't like being touched?

- Are there any words that you do/don't like to be used during sex?

- What would you like to do?

- What would you absolutely rule out?

- Are you looking for a one-off or a regular arrangement?

- Are you in a relationship and, if so, is your partner likely to have an issue with what we're doing? (You don't want a jealous boy/girlfriend turning up and ruining the vibe.)

- Have you done it before? (To establish whether someone is living out a fantasy and, as such, more likely to be nervous.)

Once you know the answers to these questions, you'll have a good idea of whether or not the threesome is likely to work. It's also worth agreeing a safe word that any one of you can use at any point if you feel uncomfortable, and establishing that all three of you will respect that. Being the third party in a threesome can be daunting, and it's important that whoever joins you feels as much a part of the process as you and your partner.

After all, it's not just your own sexual pleasure that's important: everyone involved in a sexual experience should feel comfortable, happy and, with any luck, sated by it. And with enough communication beforehand, there's no reason why this shouldn't be the case.

Swinging, Orgies and Sex Parties

Of course, you may decide that one extra person simply isn't enough when it comes to group sex. Luckily, there are plenty of places where you can play should you want to take your fantasies out of the bedroom and into a more public forum.

While the group-sex scene is by no means as large as tabloid newspapers may have you believe, according to Queendom.com about 25 per cent of men and women have fantasised about watching their partner have sex with someone else, 25 per cent of women and 44 per cent of men find the idea of watching other couples get it on arousing and about a third of women and over half of the male population find the idea of watching two women having sex a massive turn-on (no big surprise there), so it's certainly something that has an appeal for many people.

Finding an event

Although group sex still has a bit of a seedy reputation, with many people imagining it to entail obese couples getting naked in suburban houses with pampas grass on the lawn to indicate their affiliation, this is nothing like the real scene today. There are sex parties for people of all ages and body types. Some party organisers insist on seeing a photograph of attendees before they're given the location of the party, to ensure that everyone is attractive, while others may pick people based on the size of their pay packet. And some don't care about the size of your wallet, as long as the man's packet is bulging.

Search around on the Internet and you're sure to find a sex party in your area that will cater for your particular preferences and quirks. Some are themed towards certain fetishes or dress codes and some have an 'anything goes' policy. But regardless of the kind of party that you're looking for, make sure you know the answers to the following questions before deciding whether or not you're going to attend:

- **Who is arranging the event?** Some people arrange sex events on a regular basis. Others decide to simply throw a party and advertise it on the Internet in the hope of attracting like-minded couples. If you're a first-timer, it's best to go along to a more organised event; they're likely to have a more relaxed feel, clearly set out ground rules and be generally safer. Look out for themed fetish nights in clubs as a starting position and only attend a house party once you've got used to the scene. The fetish world is very friendly and it's highly likely you'll meet people at the event who can point you in the right direction. And it's always more fun going to a party when you know at least some of the people who'll be there.

  Don't be offended if you ask the organiser for their full name, and they refuse. It doesn't mean that they're being shady. It's just that arranging sex parties is still a grey area in legal terms, so people like to protect their identity. For similar reasons, you may find that you have to sign up on a website and only find out the venue location on the night of the party, via email or text message. As long as they're happy to answer any safety questions you have, you should be fine.

- **What are the ground rules for the event and are they clearly listed on the website?** Any good fetish event should have clearly stated guidelines on its website. These can include anything from dress code to rules of play (for example, no using whips anywhere other than the dungeon area). If you can't find any guidelines on the site, but still have a good feeling about the event, email the organisers to ask them for a set of rules. Generally, you'll be safer at a fetish event than at a 'normal' club because people take the ground rules more seriously. However, if you can't find an email or phone contact, don't go to the event. Even though people often mask their full names because of the stigma that swinging still has, if you can't get in touch with anyone before the event or have some form of contact from the organisers, you could be putting yourself at risk by attending.

  Note: the club's ground rules should be an addition to your own set, not a replacement. Even if there's a huge list of regulations that you need to follow at the event, you should still sit down with your partner before you attend the party and establish your own sets of rules (such as only touching each other, leaving if either of you feels uncomfortable or only having sex in public if you've both agreed on the people you'll allow to watch you). Rowing with your partner at sex parties is generally frowned upon, as it ruins the mood for other guests, but by ensuring you know each other's rules and stick to them, there shouldn't be any cause for disagreement.

- **Is the event for couples, single people or mixed?** Some parties are designed for singles, some for couples and some for anyone who wants to attend. Generally speaking, couples parties tend to be focused around swinging, although there shouldn't be any pressure to join in at any kind of kinky event, so there's nothing to say that you couldn't simply turn up and have sex while other couples look on, if that's an idea that gets you horny. It's worth bearing in mind that sex parties still tend to have a somewhat discriminatory policy towards single men, so if you are male and don't have a partner, you're likely to find yourself paying over the odds or barred from attending at all. The best bet for a single man who wants to go to a sex party is to take along a casual partner. However, if you do this, it's not good form to abandon them the second you get into the party and go off in search of new blood. If you pretend to be in a couple, you should act as if you're in a couple and simply use the party as an opportunity to enjoy yourselves together.

- **Are condoms provided or should I bring my own?** Any reputable sex party should have condoms readily available, but you should also take your own to be on the safe side. If you turn up at a sex party and there aren't condoms anywhere to be seen, it's a sign that the event isn't necessarily ideal, and you should consider whether you really want to stay.

Once you've asked all the necessary questions (and got the right answers), there's nothing to stand in your way, and there should be a reasonable number of clubs to choose from. There are thousands of perfectly safe and enjoyable swinging clubs out there, and although there do tend to be more in cities, you'd be surprised at how many suburbs boast a thriving swinging scene.

Having made your choice, you may start to feel nervous about what you've let yourself in for, but there really is no need for concern. While some people do enjoy the 'free for all' that is potentially available at sex parties, at least as many go along to chat to like-minded couples and find people who they get on with. Only after a lot of conversation will things turn sexual; after all, just because someone's into swinging, it doesn't mean that they don't have any sexual standards.

TALES FROM THE SCENE: *MANAGE YOUR EXPECTATIONS*

There's a naive popular assumption that in an orgy 'everything goes'. It's not quite like that in real life. On the bed at an orgy, unless you land on it with people who are obviously expecting to have sex with you, you have to get permission to have sex with someone. You can do that by touching them, even in intimate areas, but if they move your hand or mouth or move away, it is over. Getting on the bed does not signal availability to everyone there. In group sex the rules are different. There are not 'no rules'. There can be perfect orgies where everyone is up for sexual contact with everyone else. These are usually small parties where everyone knows everyone else and may have had sex already. As you acquire experience, it's a good idea to build a network of group-sex friends whom you like and trust and are comfortable having repeat sex with. And when you have enough of them (four or five couples), you can throw a perfect orgy yourself. They are the hottest experiences you can imagine.

Mark Roberts, organising secretary of Fever swinging events

On the day

When the day of the event arrives one of you may change your mind about going, in which case make sure you discuss this and consider cancelling. There's no point attending something that's going to make you feel uncomfortable, and you could well find that you feel differently once you've had more time to think about things. Alternatively, you may find yourself feeling frisky all day at the thought of what you're going to do. If so, it's time to start making your preparations.

Whether or not you're intending to play, make sure that you're clean and well groomed: you want to be suitable for seduction, should you change your mind. Cut your fingernails so that you don't scratch anyone, and don't forget your toenails either. Trimming back your pubes will make oral sex easier, and taking along a goodie bag packed with condoms (flavoured are best if you're likely to end up having oral sex after you've had penetrative sex), lubricant (again, flavoured is best) and any preferred sex toys (covered with a condom if you use them with anyone else) is essential. A woman should avoid using spermicidal jelly as it tastes disgusting for anyone performing cunnilingus on her; men should forgo underpants, as it's hard to get out of them sexily and they'll be able to get stuck in without any clumsiness should they decide that's what they and their partner both want. Jewellery should also be avoided, including watches, as they could scratch people or get lost (it's hard to keep track of your belongings when in the middle of a group romp).

When you first arrive at the party, allow time to familiarise yourself with the venue and generally get settled in. Spending the first hour simply wandering around, checking the various rooms and making polite conversation with other guests should help you relax, making for a better sexual experience if you do take things further.

After that first hour, find somewhere to be alone with your

partner and talk about the way that you're feeling. If either partner feels uncomfortable, leave. If not, discuss what you'd like to do. Bear in mind that if you start getting it on with your partner, you may well be approached by other people who want to join in, but a polite refusal is perfectly acceptable if you don't want them to. If someone is overly persistent, tell one of the organisers and they'll soon get kicked out.

Conversely, if you want to join in with another couple's games, don't be afraid to ask, but don't feel offended if they decline. No one should be expected to have sex with someone else, even if they are at a sex party. Some clubs have a rule that only women are allowed to make approaches, so make sure you follow the procedure if that is the case.

If you go to a party and don't see anyone that you fancy, don't get too disheartened. However, try not to be too judgemental. Spend time chatting to people and you may well find that your perception of people changes: the woman you discounted at first sight because she seemed a little overweight may be sexy as hell when you speak to her; or the man with the tiny todger could have a voice that makes you instantly wet and a tongue that could wrestle an octopus and win.

After the party, talk to your lover once more. Concerns may only arise the morning after, particularly if you had a few drinks at the party before you started playing. However, as long as neither of you is accusatory and if, instead, you talk through any issues like adults, resolve them and learn from the experience, there's no reason why they should cause problems, as long as you've followed all the guidelines above.

Of course, you might find that once you've had group sex, you're both hornier than you've ever been before and end up with a reinvigorated sex life for months afterwards. And that's what sexual experimentation is all about.

TALES FROM THE SCENE: WHY SWING?

Swinging satisfies the desire/need for sexual variety that destabilises and destroys so many long-term relationships, despite them being happy in other ways. It allows partners to hone and show off their sexual skills, learn new ones and reaffirm their desirability to each other. As a secret other life, swinging creates the exciting effect of having an affair – except that both partners are involved together. In relationships where sex has attenuated after the honeymoon phase, it provides agreed, controlled access to sex in the context of the relationship – which can often lead to a revival of sex within the relationship itself. In relationships where one partner has much more experience (perhaps the other partner had a demanding job, was religious or is simply a lot younger), it allows the other partner to 'catch up' on sexual experience without excluding their current partner. In relationships where both partners have highly promiscuous pasts or records of cheating on partners, it allows them to manage their inclinations on a mutually agreed inclusive basis to stop the relationship flying apart. It means they can have a successful long-term relationship without having to change their personalities first (which almost always fails).

In relationships where only one partner is highly sexed, has a very promiscuous past or a record of cheating, it allows the other partner to permit them controlled access to sexual variety through the relationship; regulating it on a negotiated basis and removing the possibility that it could lead to an alternative emotional attachment (because people at swingers' events are with their partners and are not emotionally available, which need not be the case with a fling at work or at the gym).

In relationships where one partner has a sexual desire or need that cannot be met by the other partner alone, it empowers the other partner to allow access to that need on an agreed basis within the relationship. This might be a desire for group sex (obviously), certain types of sex, people of a certain skin colour, physical characteristic or character type.

The key thing is that because swinging is done by couples, it is the other partner who controls access. As in the last point, for the driven partner it will always be easier to gain what she/he needs through swinging via the relationship than to find it elsewhere. Swinging is the only environment in which bisexual women can achieve sexual fulfilment. Ninety per cent plus of females in swinging relationships are (physically, if not emotionally) bisexual. It increases your satisfaction and confidence in life generally. Few people you meet have as good a sex life as you. The unfulfilled hankerings for sexual variety, hidden crushes and suppressed longings of normal life do not build up inside you. It makes it easier to be well balanced and concentrate on things other than sex.

Mark Roberts, organising secretary of Fever swinging events

Conclusion

With any luck, if you've read this book cover to cover, you should have discovered at least a few things to add an extra bit of spice to your sex life. Of course, you may also have read about some things that made you giggle, squirm or go 'Yuk'. But that's the thing with fetishes: each to their own. There's no such thing as a good or bad fetish, just kinks that simply are to your taste or not.

When it comes to sex, normal isn't something that can really be quantified and certainly isn't something to aspire to. Everyone has their own desires and quirks, and few people are honest enough to admit their more unusual desires (except, perhaps, to a partner) so there's no real way to know what 'normal' bedroom behaviour actually is. As such, there's no reason to feel ashamed about living out *your* fantasies, as long as you make sure that anything you do is safe, sane and consensual.

Conversely, you don't have to indulge every fetish that you fantasise about. Sometimes it can be fun to have private turnons that exist merely in your own head and make it easier for you to come. While it can be easy to fall into the trap of trying new things because the media says it's the latest thing in Hollywood, having a tick-list approach to sexuality isn't necessary – or particularly likely to lead to sexual enlightenment. Before you try anything new, think about whether it's something you actually want to do or whether you're responding to pressure from your partner, the media or society in general. You can always 'try on' a fetish by fantasising about it for a while to see whether it's something that you'd really like to experience.

The most important thing is to make sure that you keep your mind open, both towards your own desires and those that your partner chooses to share with you. Even though a fetish may do nothing for you now, that doesn't mean it won't in a few years' time; and conversely, just because you have discovered a penchant for a new kink, that doesn't mean you're necessarily tied to it for life. Sexuality is fluid and you may well find that your kinks evolve as you get older and your life experiences change. There are certainly things I've tried and enjoyed that I would have never imagined would be fun when I was younger; and fantasies that I've lived out only to discover they were no big deal, after all. But every one of them has been a learning experience, and there's nothing I've tried in the fetish world that I regret because it really is a fabulously open, kind and welcoming place to hang out.

Exploring your fetishes can be a good way to learn not just about your sexuality, but also yourself. Assuming different power roles can help you come to terms with low self-esteem or control issues. Dressing up in different costumes can help bring different aspects of your personality to the fore. Allowing yourself to be vulnerable can help strengthen your relationship with your partner. These are just a few of the ways that experimenting sexually can help you grow as a person. So, enjoy delving into your dark side, safe in the knowledge that it's probably helping you become more self-aware. Just remember the golden rule – keep it friendly.

Resources

If you've enjoyed reading *Friendly Fetish*, you may want to research the area further and discover more about what turns you on. If you're after erotic inspiration (aka bedtime reading) there are numerous publishers producing contemporary anthologies. Cleis Press and Cheek both produce some great books in the US, while Xcite Books, Black Lace and Nexus lead the way in the UK. Some anthologies are themed, with every story focusing around, say, BDSM, while others cover the full gamut of fetish.

Unsurprisingly, there is also a vast array of websites offering erotic stories, videos or both. JanesGuide.com is a fantastic review-based site that will help you work through the wealth of material available to find something that will turn you on. In addition, the following resources may prove useful if you're after something more specific:

Books

***Delta of Venus*, Anaïs Nin (Penguin Modern Classics, 2000)** As one of the first women to produce erotica for a mass market, Nin covers a variety of themes from sensual orgies to evocative exhibitionistic daydreams, all written in beautifully flowing prose.

***Erotic Home Video: Create Your Own Adult Films,* Anna Span (Carlton Books, 2003)** A well-informed and easy-to-follow guide to erotic filmmaking from Europe's leading female porn producer and director, Anna Span.

***Fetish Fact Book,* The, Paul Scott (Virgin Books, 2004)** Toilet book with a fetish theme – full of fascinating facts about fetish.

***Fork Me, Spoon Me: An Aphrodisiac Cookbook,* Amy Reiley and Kersti Frigell (Life of Reiley, 2006)** A cute and quirky guide to aphrodisiac cooking.

***My Secret Garden,* Nancy Friday (Quartet Books, 2001)** Although this was written as an academic study into the female erotic imagination, Friday includes transcripts of hundreds of genuine sexual fantasies from women, so it works equally well as inspirational material. The book was a huge success, and was followed by more of the same, including *Men in Love* (Arrow Books, 2003) which details male sexual fantasies. It's highly likely that you will find at least one fantasy to turn you on among the hundreds that Friday found over the years.

***Naughty Spanking Stories,* edited by Miranda Forbes (Xcite Books, 2008)** A hot anthology of erotic stories with a spanking theme.

***Private Thoughts: Exploring the Power of Women's Sexual Fantasies,* Suzie Boss and Wendy Maltz (New World Library, 2001)** Fascinating insight into female sexual fantasies.

True Confessions of a London Spank Daddy, The, **Peter Jones (Xcite Books, 2008)** Sex memoir written by a man who spanks women for a living.

Websites

Adultfriendfinder.com Contact website that allows you to search for other people to play with. It's also great for finding fetishists of every type imaginable.

Cliterati.co.uk An erotic story website that offers a range of fantasies including straight, gay, sub/Dom, group and 'taboo'. Anyone can add a story, so you can share your fantasies with the world, as well as reading other people's.

Dirtymoviesforgirls.com Similar to Strictlybroadband, but this site's content is tailored for women.

Literotica.com Another broad-ranging site with a particularly impressive collection of fetish stories. Again, you can add your own fantasies to the site, if the idea turns you on.

Pornotube.com Porn website offering free content and giving you the opportunity to add your own footage to the site, should you so wish.

Scarleteen.com Great resource designed for teens, but well worth reading if you're after sexual health, sexuality and sexual politics advice.

Sexplained.com Everything you need to know about safer sex.

Strictlybroadband.com Streamed porn videos on demand, allowing you to sift through thousands of titles and find something that will turn you both on.

DVDs

A&O Department A sexy, female-friendly porn film with a doctors-and-nurses theme from award-winning director (including an award in the International Emma Feminist Porn Awards) Anna Span.

Cooking With Aphrodisiacs Learn how to make twenty recipes using sixteen different aphrodisiac foodstuffs. Also includes information on how to make aphrodisiac drinks.

Female Fantasies A sensual video depicting numerous female fantasies, from female porn producer and director Petra Joy.

Sex Shops and Fetish Stockists

Ann Summers One of the biggest sex brands in the world, selling fantasy outfits, lingerie, sex toys and fetish props. Stores in the UK, Ireland and Spain. Also available online at www.annsummers.com.

Coco de Mer Designer sex store with shops in Melrose Avenue, New York and Covent Garden, London. Also available online at www.coco-de-mer.com. Sells a great range of toys, from discreet vibrators for beginners to horsetail whips, crystal butt plugs complete with tails, corsets, play outfits and numerous other kinky items.

Femplay.co.uk/au Female-targeted Australian sex shop with sex toys, pubic shavers and generally kinky items.

Fetteredpleasures.com Bondage and fetish website selling whips, chains, fetish clothing, pony and puppy play accessories and a host of other kinky treats.

Funtasia.com/au Australian sex shop featuring sex toys and fetish gear of all kinds.

Nzadulttoys.co.nz New Zealand sex store packed with bondage kit, sexy books, sex toys and more.

OnJoy.com Comprehensive, reliable and discreet female-friendly sex toy website which also stocks a number of role-play outfits.

She Said Gorgeous designer boutique in Brighton, UK, with trained corset fitters and a host of sex toys and kinky items. Also available online at www.shesaidboutique.com.

Index

9½ *Weeks* (1986) 108

accessories 47–51
  see also fashion; furniture, kinky;
    sex toys
alcohol consumption 186
ampallang 175, 176
anal beads 138–9, 145
anal sex 42, 223–4
anal stimulation, sex toys for 144–7
anal stretchers 145
analingus 223–4
ankle restraints 208
apadravya 175, 176–7
aphrodisiacs 92, 97–104, 108–9
asparagus 98
  with melted butter 102
asphyxiation 200
Attree, Michael 'Atters' 192
audiences, performing for 85–9

Babestation 22–3
Ball Bras 126
bananas 98
BDSM (bondage and discipline,
    dominance and submission,
    and sadism and masochism)
    5, 215–42
  bondage 197–214
  masochists 234
  sadists 234

spanking 183–96
sub/Dom play 117–18, 182,
  215–42
bicuriousity 73–6, 243, 251
bisexuality 252, 266
blindfolds 189
blinis, caviar and sour cream 101
body care 130–4
body modification 168–81
bondage 197–214
  and alcohol consumption 201
  Japanese rope 202, 203, 210–13
  mild 197–8, 205
  neck care 200
  restraints 197–8, 200–3, 205–9
  risks 199–204, 231–2
  suspension 202, 211
  techniques 205–10
  vore play 119–20
  see also BDSM
bondage tape 200
books, erotic 17–18, 48–9
boot fetishism 157–8
Boss, Suzie 44–5
branding 170–1, 181
burlesque 59–60
butt plugs 135, 145

camera phones 28
canapés 108–9
'cannibalistic' fetishes 119–21

carrots 98
'caught in the act' (game) 73–5
caviar and sour cream blinis 101
celery soup with white truffle oil 99
chastity belts 224–6
   male 224–6
chilli 98, 101, 117
chocolate 98
   dark chocolate mousse 100
Christina (piercing) 178
clam and saffron linguini 104
clitoral hood, piercing 175, 178–80
clitoral stimulation, sex toys for
   140–1
clitoris, piercing 178
clubs
   female domination 2–3, 235–6
   fetish 85–6
   lap-dancing 61–2
cock rings 138–9
condoms 261, 263
corsets 125, 161–5
counsellors 9
couples parties 260–1, 264
crème brûlée, honey and lavender
   103
cunnilingus 263
custard wrestling 114–16
cybersex 30–6, 46
cystitis 142–3

dancing
   'private dancer' (game) 41–2,
      76–80
   see also discos, naked; pole-
      dancing; striptease
defining fetish 4–5
dental dams 223–4
depilatory creams 133–4
'dinner's on me' 104–7
directors, female 49, 54

discos, naked 2, 83–4
dogging 80
Dolphin 177
Dom/sub play *see* sub/Dom play
double penetration (DP) 251
dungeons, hiring 228
Dydoe 177

Easton, Dossie 44, 51, 157, 161,
   199, 210, 211
ejaculation 148
Ellis, Bruce 12
endorphin release
   and pain play 234
   passing out and 231
   spanking and 183–4, 186–8,
      191–3
   and tattoos 172
erections, shots of (Mull of Kintyre
   rule) 54
erotic books 17–18, 48–9
erotic films 49
erotic writing 18, 37–8
exhibitionism 53–90, 107
   games 76–89
   risks of 57–8
   sharing with your partner 58–9
   true confessions of 56, 87–9
eye contact 78

fantasies 11–52
   accessories for 47–51
   common 11–12
   cybersex 30–3, 46
   defining 12–13
   embarrassment/guilt about 16
   enacting 38–40
   and erotic writing 18, 37–8, 46
   of group sex 249–50
   and masturbation 5
   over-reliance on 43

fantasies – *contd*
  and phone sex 27–30
  purpose of 14
  risks of 43–7
  and role play 40–3
  scary 26
  sharing 14–26
  true confessions of 13, 19–20,
      22–3, 26, 29–32, 35–6,
      39–42
  and trust issues 45–6
  virtual 33–6, 46
  when not to share 24–6
fashion 50–1, 123–82
  and body care 130–4
  corsets 125, 161–5
  getting stuck in 235–6
  for kitten play 168
  lingerie 125–30
  for pony play 166–8
  for puppy play 168
  rubber, leather and PVC
      158–61
  shoe/boot fetishism 157–8
  slave clothing 224
  for submissives 224–6
  true confessions regarding
      128–32, 163–5, 169–74,
      180
'feed me' option 107–11
female domination clubs 2–3,
      235–6
female ejaculation 141
fetish clubs 85–6
  see also female domination clubs
figging 117–18
figs 97–8
films
  erotic 49
  see also pornography
fishnet tights 156–7

food play 91–121
  aphrodisiacs 92, 97–104, 108–9
  custard wrestling 113–16
  'dinner's on me' 104–7
  'feed me' option 107–11
  figging 116–18
  food fights 111–13
  menus 99–104
  sploshing 93, 114–16
  true confessions regarding
      109–11, 112–13, 117–18
  vore play 119–21
foot fetishes 151–8
foot rubs 152
Fourchette piercing 178
Fraser, Mat 189
frenulum 172–4, 176–8
Friday, Nancy 12–13
furniture, kinky 124, 149–51,
      190–1

G-pilot 143
G-spot stimulation, sex toys for
      140, 141–4
G-thrust 143–4
garlic 99–100
  mushroom filo parcels 103
gay pornography 55
genital piercing 172–9
  as chastity belt 225–6
  female 178–9
  male 172–4, 176–8
genital spanking 192
genital tattoos 171
ginger 98, 100, 101, 116–18
  stem, ice cream 104
Gold, Emma 187, 216
group sex 5, 243–66
  fantasies of 249–50
  risks of 246–9
  simulation 148–9

threesomes 250–8
true confessions of 253–5
Guiche piercing 178

Hafada/Hafada ladder 177
Hames, Ashley 124, 244
handcuffs 201, 207–8
hide and seek 71–3
hog-tying 119, 206–7

ice cream, stem ginger 104
Internet, broadcasting your own
    porn on 87
Isabella piercing 179

Jacob's (frenulum) ladder 177
Japanese rope bondage 202, 203,
    210–13
jealousy 74, 244, 246
Joy, Petra 54

Kama Sutra 183
Karma Sheetra 150–1
King's Cross (male piercing) 177
kitten play 125, 168

labial piercing 179
lap-dancing clubs 61–2
leather clothes 158–61
leg men 156–7
lingerie 125–30
    for men 126
    padded 126
    sizing 127
linguini, clam and saffron 104
lobster, fresh, served with rocket
    salad 99–100
Lorum ladder 177
lubricants
    and anal penetration 145
    flavoured 95–6

Maltz, Wendy 44–5
masochists 234
    see also BDSM
masturbation
    compulsive 229–30
    and fantasy 5
    in front of mirrors 65–8
    mutual 55–6, 68–73
    prevention 225–6
    and sex toys 136–7
masturbation gloves 135
masturbation sheaths 148, 149,
    249
men
    chastity belts for 224–6
    genital piercings 172–4, 176–8
    lingerie for 126
    pole dancing 80
    pubic hair care 130
    sex toys for 135–6, 138–9, 148,
        149, 249
    striptease 60, 77, 78
menus 99–104
mirrors 62–4, 65–8
Mistress Absolute 43, 86
Monet, Veronica 204
Monroe, Marilyn 157
mousse, dark chocolate 100
Mull of Kintyre rule 54
Multi-User Dimension 33
mushroom filo parcels, garlic 103

naked discos 2, 83–4
naturism 2, 82–5
Nefertiti piercing 179
Night of the Senses (sex party) 3,
    187
nipple clamps 235
nipple piercing 169–70, 181
nipple stimulation, sex toys for 144
nyotaimori 105–7

oral sex 75–6
   and piercings 173
   sprays 95–7
orgasms 137
   control of 232–4
   psycholagnic 14–15
   and spanking 192
   and sub/Dom play 209, 219,
      232–4
orgies 2, 243, 258–66
out-of-body experiences 183–4
outdoor sex 39–40, 57, 80–2
oysters 97
   fresh 103

pain 216–17
pain play 234–6
   safe words 235
paraphilias (sexual deviations) 53
parties, sex 3, 189, 258–66
passing out 231
penis 172–4, 176–8
   see also erections
personal hygiene 94, 223–4, 263
phallic symbols 97, 98
pheromones 93
phone sex 22–3, 27–30, 45
photos, erotic 28
piercings 125, 168–70, 172–81
   genital 172–9, 225–6
   nipple 169–70, 181
   and oral sex 173
   tips 174–5
pineapple 94, 98
   carpaccio 102
pole-dancing 41–2, 79–80
   male 80
pony play 125, 166–8
pornography 49, 131
   female directors 54
   gay 55
   making your own/DIY 87
   women and 53–5
   see also erotic films
Prince Albert 176
Princess Albertina 179
'private dancer' (game) 41–2,
      76–80
props 50–1, 123–82
   for foot fetishes 151–7
   kinky furniture 124, 149–51,
      190–1
   see also sex toys
'pros and cons' of kink 6–7
prostate stimulation 146–7
psycholagnic orgasm 14–15
pubic hair care 130–4
pubic piercing 178
public sex 39–40, 57, 80–2
puppy play 125, 168
PVC clothes 158–61

recipes 99–104
   asparagus with melted butter
      103
   caviar and sour cream blinis 101
   celery soup with white truffle oil
      99
   clam and saffron linguini 104
   dark chocolate mousse 100
   fresh lobster served with rocket
      salad 99–100
   fresh oysters 104
   garlic mushroom filo parcels 103
   honey and lavender crème brulée
      103
   pineapple carpaccio 102
   scallops with chilli and ginger
      101–2
   stem ginger ice cream 104
restraints 197–8, 200–3, 205–9
Roberts, Mark 245, 252, 262, 266

role play 11–52
    accessories for 47–51, 124
    defining 12–13
    and fantasies 41–3
    risks of 42–7
ropes 200–1
    silk/cotton 207
Royalle, Candida 54
rubber clothes 158–61

sadists 234
    see also BDSM
safe words/codes 46–7, 185–6,
    191–2, 219–21, 235, 239
scallops with chilli and ginger 101–2
Scarlet (magazine) 54, 96, 138
seafood 98
self-development 9
semen, sweetening 94, 98
sex dolls 136
sex lotions/potions 139–40
sex parties 3, 189, 258–66
sex swings 150
sex toys 81, 123–4, 135–49
    anal stimulation for her 144–5
    anal stimulation for him 146–7
    cautions regarding 136–7
    for clitoral stimulation 140–1
    for G-spot stimulation 140,
        141–4
    and group sex fantasies 249
    for men 135–6, 138–9, 148,
        149, 249
    for nipple stimulation 144
    oral 139
    remote-controlled 60, 139
    sharing 69, 138–9
    testing 138
    toy shows 147–9
    vibrators 135, 138–41, 151, 179

sexual deviations (paraphilias) 53
sexual injuries 94–5
sexual juices 93–7, 98
sexual persona, exploring your
    14
shaving 132–3
shoe fetishism 157–8
SKype 28
slaves
    clothing 224
    playing 226–9
    'topping from the bottom' 229
slip knots 200, 211
soup, celery, with white truffle oil
    99
Span, Anna 54
spanking 183–96
    aftercare 184, 192–3
    'come down' 192–3
    the genital area 192
    to orgasm 192
    positions for 190–1
    psychological aspects 189
    risks of 185–8
    safe words/codes for 185–6,
        191–2
    'sweet spot' 187
    techniques 188–9, 191
    true confessions regarding
        184–5, 193–5
spanking paddles 184, 195
    branded 184
Spankties 207
'spit-roasting' 251
sploshing 93, 114–16
spreader bars 208
Sprinkle, Annie 82, 92, 159, 162,
    247
strap-ons 142–3, 146–7, 224
striptease 59–61, 77–8
    male 60, 77, 78

sub/Dom play 117–18, 182,
    215–42
  bondage 214
  Doms 231–8
  legal issues 217
  and orgasms 209, 219, 232–4
  pain play 234–6
  pony play 166–8
  risks of 219–22
  role turn-taking 238–41
  safe words/codes for 46–7,
      219–21, 235, 239
  spanking 185
  submission 222–30
  and tattoos 170–1
  true confessions of 229–30,
      239–41
  vore play 119–20
  watersports 237–8
  see also BDSM
suspension bondage 202, 211
'sweet spot' 187
swinging 86, 258–66
swings 150
Symons, Donald 12

taboos 42, 57
talking dirty 20–3, 222–4

tantra 55
tattoos 168–9, 170–1
tawses 195–6
Tenga 149, 249
text-messaging 27–8
threesomes 250–8
'topping from the bottom' 229

vaginal infections 145
'vanillas' 1–2
vibrators 135, 138–41
  make-shift 151
  and piercings 179
virtual fantasies 33–6, 46
vore play 119–21
voyeurism 5, 53–90, 258
  games 59–76
  risks of 57–8
  sharing with your partner 58–9
  true confessions of 56, 61–2,
      64–5, 70, 72–3, 74–5

waist:hip ratio 161–2
watersports 237–8
waxing 134
wrestling, custard 113–16
wrist restraints 207
writing, erotic 18, 37–8